Shaping a
House for the
Church

MARCHITA MAUCK

Shaping a House for the Church

Liturgy Training Publications

Dedicated to
my Notre Dame classmates
whose love of liturgy
continues to inspire me
and whose friendship
graces my life:

E.B.,   E.F.,   E.H.,   R.H.,   S.J.,   M.L.,   D.N.,   T.R.,   T.S.

Acknowledgments for all photos and illustrations, along with reference information, will be found on the last pages of this book.

Liturgy Training Publications
1800 North Hermitage Avenue
Chicago IL 60622-1101
1-800-933-1800

Cover and book design by Ana Aguilar-Islas
Printed in the United States of America

ISBN 0-929650-06-9

CONTENTS

ACKNOWLEDGMENTS

Writing a book is a powerful experience of one's dependence on others. I began with a desire to articulate insights from my art historical and liturgical backgrounds that might form a basis for dialogue about the design of churches. The academic knowledge and reflection has been enfleshed by the experience of many people in "the trenches," my colleagues who are liturgical design consultants and those architects, designers, artists, pastors, liturgists and musicians who have so generously sent me photographs, invited me to their churches, and spent long hours discussing issues with me. The students in my classes on art and liturgy and liturgical design at the University of Notre Dame challenged me and inspired me. The communities and pastors and architects with whom I have worked on renovation and new design projects have added immeasurably to my appreciation of the complexity and gratification of designing places for worship. To all of them I am grateful.

The Ragdale Foundation of Lake Forest, Illinois, provided a residency grant for the initial commitment of chapters to computer disk. From the beginning, Gabe Huck of Liturgy Training Publications has been patient and always ready with wise counsel. Bill Beard, who does church design in Colorado Springs, was a wonderful help when the time came to edit illustrations and critique the text.

There are always people who provide a different sort of support, an ongoing confidence that the project will indeed reach closure. This day-to-day encouragement, without which one would not survive with grace and humor, came from many friends: Armando Garzon (who also provided all the drawings), Dorothy Shawhap, Don Neumann, and Bob Hutmacher. Finally, thanks to my family and my two soul friends who have born the brunt of all the highs and lows of this and all my projects, Dan Drinan and John Edmunds.

PREFACE

This book proposes that a church building has a double responsibility. It must both reflect and form a people. The place itself shares the mission of the liturgical assembly to be sign, witness and instrument of the reign of God.[1] Well-designed liturgical spaces lead the church to renewed insight into its nature. Those charged with shaping such places have a responsibility, and indeed mission, to provide designs affirming the church's contemporary understanding of itself.

The *Constitution on the Sacred Liturgy* was promulgated in 1963, the first document of Vatican II. Taking first things first, the world's bishops called for full, conscious and active participation in the liturgy, so that identity as community would permeate the faithful and have consequences in the larger world.

All who have concern and responsibility for the place of liturgy must look at exactly *what* the assembly does, at its rites and how and why they are celebrated. The actions of the worshiping assembly represent generations of reflection. They are characterized by centuries of development and evolution to meet changing needs. It is those actions that must shape the house for the church.

This book is intended for pastors and building committees, architects, artists and all who become involved in the designing or renovation of places for worship.

Although the author's point of view is Roman Catholic, it is hoped that the methodology and principles invoked will provide insight for all who struggle with the noble task of designing worship places.

Notes:

1. *Environment and Art in Catholic Worship* [EACW], Bishops' Committee on the Liturgy (Washington, D.C.: National Conference of Catholic Bishops, 1978), 38.

   The Bishops' Committee document is quoted throughout this book. In the face of questions concerning this document's authority, the U.S. Bishops' Committee on the Liturgy clarified its position in the Committee's August/September 1985, *Newsletter.* It stated:

   In 1978 EACW was published. As an explicitation of the norms of the *General Instruction of the Roman Missal* (Chapter V), EACW has the force of particular law in the dioceses of the United States. It expands those norms and sets policy for building, renovation, decoration, and furnishing of churches.

CHAPTER **1**

The Liturgical Environment

DOES ANYONE HAVE the foggiest idea what sort of power we so blithely invoke? . . . It is madness to wear ladies' straw hats and velvet hats to church; we should all be wearing crash helmets. Ushers should issue life preservers and signal flares; they should lash us to our pews. For the sleeping god may wake someday and take offense, or the waking god may draw us out to where we can never return.[1]

Annie Dillard's boat-rocking metaphor confronts one with the nature of encounters with God. She speaks of the awesome potential of ritual to mediate the presence of the Lord. The church challenges Christians to allow the Lord's transforming power to take hold of their lives. To do so is to be changed. Allowing oneself to be formed anew includes the probability that God just may "draw us out to where we can never return."

The *Constitution on the Sacred Liturgy* says the same thing in its own way:

The liturgy in its turn moves the faithful, filled with "the paschal sacraments," to be "one in holiness"; it prays that "they may hold fast in their lives to what they have grasped by their faith"; the renewal in the eucharist of the covenant between the Lord and his people draws the faithful into the compelling love of Christ and sets them on fire.[2]

The imagery of both texts is dramatic. The storm-tossed boat washed out into unknown territory and the vision of being set afire convey the impelling force of God's activity. This activity of God is transforming and has consequences. People who are drawn out to where they cannot return have a new perspective. They have to make decisions about new directions. They need to be acutely aware of where they've been and sensitive to the options they see before them. They will understand that they are moving, "on pilgrimage" as the church describes herself.[3] Christians at liturgy cannot be spectators at a dramatic presentation. They are the protagonists of the story.

Full, conscious, active participation in the liturgy by all believers is essential for being church. Although Christians are called also to private prayer, the *Constitution on the Sacred Liturgy* calls participation in the public prayer of the church "the primary and indispensable source from which the faithful are to derive the true Christian spirit."[4] The environment is to support and enhance the liturgy. It should beckon people, exhort them, guide them, lift their spirits and help bring them into encounters with others and with the Lord.

Qualities of the Environment

Environment and Art in Catholic Worship speaks of the worship environment as a "serving environment." We are to look for this in "the character of a particular space and how it affects the action of the assembly."[5] The environment is expected to play an active role. It is never a backdrop in front of which other things happen.

Buildings have personalities. E. A. Sovik observes: "Buildings can be described in the same terms as people can: they can be noble, trivial, awkward, vigorous, charming; they can be domineering, imposing, boring, peremptory."[6] The personality of the place can either promote or hinder what is done there. About churches, Sovik questions: "Does this thing convey the truth? Does it speak about something relevant and consequential?"[7]

The truth that seeks expression is the revelation of who we are as assembled Christians, a people who embrace the incarnation and its consequences. We need environments to affirm the holy actions in which we participate. A place for worship is not a sacred place of its own accord. It is effective only insofar as it supports the actions of the people. Sovik aptly points out:

> A church building that seeks consciously to induce what used to be called the "mood of worship" is suspect because it seeks to manipulate. If a building is to be an image of love, the words that might be used to describe it would be words like gracious, companionable, generous, strong, gentle and hospitable.[8]

The more we understand about the evocative and provocative power of images, the more cognizant we become of the need for clarity about who we are and what we do. Only then can we shape an environment that bespeaks the truths that are important to us, both for the outsider observing us and for ourselves, so that by repetitive reinforcement we may ever become more what we already are.

Formative Characteristics

Christians gather. That simple truth has implications. Is there a hospitable gathering place encouraging us to visit, to enter, to linger? Or do the doors of the church empty out into vistas of asphalt parking lots? Is the gathering place available at other times during the week for visitors, for neighbors? Is it a place for parents and young children to rest, for the elderly to visit?

When we enter a church, what is to be seen? Do we recognize that here is a baptizing, reconciling community that gathers at the eucharistic table? Or does it rather appear that this is a place where lots of people probably come to sit down and watch any number of things occur up front? Do we discover a font so built and so located that we understand that the people of the community stand with awe before baptism's wondrous power?

Would we then find evidence that the community is one of reconciliation? This is not just a matter of some effective public relations work for a languishing sacrament. It is a question of how we ourselves are formed into people who both need reconciliation and who need to be reconcilers. Do we see, near the gathering spaces, reconciliation places that convey welcome and graciousness? Would we feel differently about reconciliation if it were an ever present part of the hospitality we extend to each other?

To celebrate eucharist is to gather as guests at the table of the Lord. Do we understand that to celebrate eucharist is to give assent to a habit of being that continually needs practice so that we may be renewed and nourished as a holy people?

To participate in the life of Christ cannot be accomplished by sitting in a pew and admiring the flowers. It can only occur as Christians make the journey through the waters of baptism and return home again and again to be forgiven and to be nourished at the table of the Lord's banquet.

Conclusion

The environment is to offer such hospitality, to accord dignity to all and to invite all to journey. The journey involves recalling and practicing who the assembly is: the body of Christ. Part of the process requires experiencing, perhaps in a somewhat larger than life way, familiar actions and gestures. The evocative and provocative power of the familiar rises up and transcends the ordinary, requiring attentiveness and response.

Liturgy enlarges familiar gestures and actions so that they take on new life and so that people become aware of them as constitutive of all parts of their lives. Liturgy demands spaces capable of bearing the weight of mystery as well as capable of embracing all of what it means to be human.

There is no more legitimate source for the shape of the worship place than the shape of what happens there. Ritual actions should shape the worship place so that it, in turn, can shape and support and enhance those actions. It is the actions of ritual that mediate the holy. Christ's presence and activity in the assembly, in the word, in the minister and in the eucharist are the source of the transformation of people's lives.[9]

The actions shaping the worship place flow sequentially and will be considered in the remaining chapters:

CHAPTER 2 Gathering
CHAPTER 3 Entering and Going Forth
CHAPTER 4 Initiation and Reconciliation
CHAPTER 5 Eucharist
CHAPTER 6 Art in the Service of Worship

Notes:

1. Annie Dillard, *Teaching a Stone to Talk* (New York: Harper Colophon Books, 1982), 41–42.

2. *Constitution on the Sacred Liturgy*, 100. *Documents on the Liturgy* (Collegeville: The Liturgical Press, 1982). Hereafter quoted as DOL.

3. *Dogmatic Constitution on the Church*, chapter 7.

4. *Constitution on the Sacred Liturgy*, 14.

5. *Environment and Art in Catholic Worship* (Washington, D.C.: National Conference of Catholic Bishops, 1978), 24. Hereafter cited as EACW.

6. E. A. Sovik, "Notes on Sacred Space," *The Christian Century* (March 31, 1982), 363.

7. Sovik, *Architecture for Worship* (Minneapolis: Augsburg Publishing House, 1973), 47.

8. Sovik, "Notes on Sacred Space," 365.

9. *Constitution on the Sacred Liturgy*, 7.

CHAPTER **2**

Gathering

SUPPOSE YOU WERE a grocer in Brondesbury, a tradesman in a small way of business, as so many of the early Roman Christians were. Week by week at half-past four or five o'clock on Sunday morning (an ordinary working day in pagan Rome) before most people were stirring, you would set out through the silent streets.[1]

When Dom Gregory Dix interpreted in a modern setting an early Christian eucharist in Rome, he began with the image of the grocer in Brondesbury setting out through the silent streets very early on a Sunday morning. The gathering of the assembly begins when people leave their own homes.

For Christians in pagan Rome, to gather for eucharist was a risky business. Discovery carried with it the possibility of death. In times of persecution, Christians would have moved through the predawn streets to the place for the celebration of eucharist only if participation meant as much as life itself.

Gathering for worship in twentieth-century America seems a messier, less decisive matter. A hasty departure from home is more likely the result of dawdling over the Sunday paper than of any apprehension about being publicly recognized en route as a Christian. If one arrives at church in some emotional disarray, the reason probably has to do with children having left things that had to be retrieved, or arguments with teenagers who do not want to come at all, or any of a hundred other lesser or greater aggravations making a shambles of one's serenity.

Implications of Gathering

Ultimately, we decide to come to worship with others because "we are summoned to appear before the God of all the earth and to do our priestly duty in Christ on behalf of all humanity."[2] Somehow there must be a transformation of the external noisiness at the beginning of the journey into an inner openness and quiet at the end. Each person must see himself or herself as privileged and summoned to join with others and contribute who they are to the harmony and unity of the whole gathered body of Christ.

We are summoned by the same invitation as were those early Roman Christians. God continues to gather a people. Convening the church remains God's initiative. The approach of people of all ages and shapes and colors and social classes from all directions offers an animated and stirring image of God's continuing activity. What a motley crew the Lord brings home! A moment for revelation surely vanishes if people enter a church from a parking lot without having the opportunity to bump into each other and remind themselves they have come, along with all those others, at the Lord's invitation. How satisfying an ample, generous, hospitable area for convening—a "gathering place"—might be as image of the Lord's invitation.

In twelfth- and thirteenth-century Europe, the entrance portal to churches often included a life-size statue of Christ standing in the middle of the doorway. (Figure 1) The worshiper would not have missed the point that Christ is the host, graciously awaiting the guests. As St. Augustine put it, "He stood in the door because by him we come unto the Father and without him we cannot enter the City of God."[3] Such an image is not a part of our familiar visual tradition, but modern believers too could respond to expressions conveying that the body of Christ anticipates and expects their presence.

The gathering place for the church is to demonstrate that

1. Christ is the host convening God's people.

God's people are expected. The entrance rite has already begun in people's departure from their homes and movement toward the church. The process of coming together is the beginning of worship. A gathering place is a presumption that the Lord is already busy among us as we recognize and greet one another.

The incorporation of a gathering place in the design of Christian churches is as old as Christian architecture. Large open courtyards preceded the great fourth-century churches in Rome, such as St. Peter's, built under the patronage of the Emperor Constantine. (Figure 2) Constantine declared the official toleration of all religions, including Christianity, early in the fourth century, giving Christians their first opportunity to construct public buildings for worship.

2. Gathering places are part of our tradition.

Historical Development

The courtyard, or atrium, was intended for the purpose of gathering and welcoming. This is known from both the history of the space as an architectural form and from early references to fountains and other provisions for pilgrims and visitors. A rectangular building, called a basilica, was adapted for Christian use. Basilicas were civic structures, often located adjacent to a public forum or open marketplace.

3. Roman civic basilica.

4. Early Christian adaptation of Roman basilica plan.

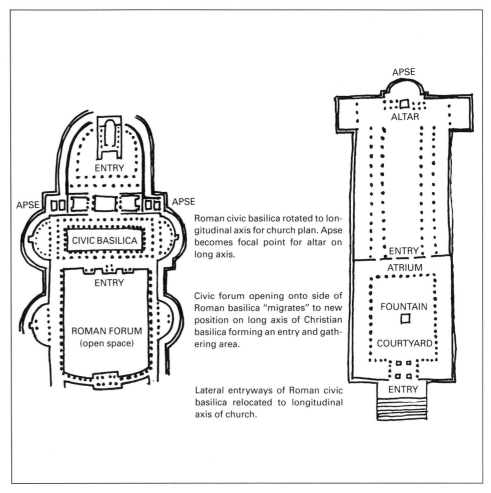

Roman civic basilica rotated to longitudinal axis for church plan. Apse becomes focal point for altar on long axis.

Civic forum opening onto side of Roman basilica "migrates" to new position on long axis of Christian basilica forming an entry and gathering area.

Lateral entryways of Roman civic basilica relocated to longitudinal axis of church.

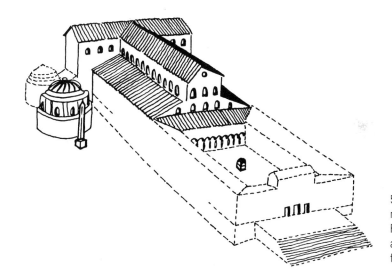

5. The animated public marketplace of the Roman forum became an open couryard in front of churches.

was a place of social interchange, now was suitably modified to meet the need for a similar gathering place before a church building.

A large fountain, placed at St. Peter's in the second half of the fourth century by Pope Damasus, became the centerpiece of the atrium at St. Peter's.

> Beneath a glittering bronze cupola, raised on slender columns of antique porphyry, stood the great gilded bronze pinecone from the top of the Emperor Hadrian's mausoleum. Through apertures in the pinecone and from the beaks of gilded peacocks the water gushed, to fall into a shallow basin intended for the ablutions of the faithful entering the basilica.[5]

Although the fountain was later dismantled and the bronze pinecone was moved into one of the courtyards of the Vatican palace, sixteenth-century drawings showing the fountain indicate the splendid focus it provided.

The long side of the building fronted the forum and had an entrance that afforded access. (Figure 3) A longitudinal or processional axis proved more functional for the celebration of Christian liturgies. The entrance was shifted from the long side to one end, facing the apse at the opposite end, a semicircular niche-like shape in front of which the altar was located. (Figures 4 and 5) Architectural historian Richard Krautheimer suggests that "the forum itself, which in most cases had been on the long side, migrated to the small side and became the atrium."[4] Thus a space which originally functioned as the marketplace in which people congregated, greeted each other, and

6. The church reaches out to embrace the people.

The welcoming of visitors continued to be a concern in subsequent times. In the sixth century, Pope Symmachus provided "housing for the poor, pilgrims' hostels rather than almshouses; and, on the piazza, facing the church and obviously for pilgrims, he set up a fountain and a lavatory."[6] The cool, flowing water of countless fountains throughout the city continues to this day to delight and refresh visitors to Rome. (We have a modern remembrance, laconic at best, of the fountain as part of the welcome to pilgrims at St. Peter's and other early Christian churches. Those holy water fonts at the doors of churches are the minimalist descendants of the early Christian fountains![7])

The much later piazza at St. Peter's comes to mind as the most familiar image of an expansive embrace. (Figure 6) Many have experienced being drawn into the church through the atrium formed by the enormous curved colonnades flanking the piazza. The baroque architect Bernini, who designed that courtyard in the middle of the seventeenth century, was well aware of the symbolic value of the space he shaped. He compared the colonnades to the maternal arms of the church that "embrace Catholics so as to confirm them in their faith; heretics, to reunite them to the church; and infidels, to enlighten them in the true faith."[8]

Bernini's image of the colonnaded atrium is human, maternal. It beckons, embraces and invites people to approach the portal with anticipation. The gradual narrowing of the space as one nears the front of the building funnels people closer together and increases a sense of uniting with so many diverse others. The distance across the great piazza followed by the gradual ascent of the many steps seems to demand a letting go of other concerns to focus upon the journey toward the great doors and entry into the sanctuary beyond.

A Modern Example

A modern example of the concept of gathering as a transitional process, not unlike that discovered in Bernini's piazza at St. Peter's in

Rome, is the design of the site at the former Dominican liturgy center in Sante Fe, New Mexico. Artist Barbara Schmich describes the experience of approaching the church there:

> The parking lot is deliberately placed at a fair distance from the building. The two are connected by a narrow path bordered by sagebrush and desert flowers and some simple stations of the cross. The path is uphill a good portion of the way and in the simple act of attending to where one is going one sees Monte del Sol, the tallest peak of the Sangre de Cristo mountains. A turn toward the left takes one into a rather narrow passageway which gradually yields up its meaning: it is like the outer layer of a shell, spiraling toward the central worship space. In this passageway are items of spiritual interest placed at various points for people to stop and ponder. Immediately before entering the worship space, there is a display of sacred art pertinent to the liturgy of the day. Father Blase Shauer, OP, director of the community, said the walk is meant to last 25 minutes.[9]

7. A processional path heightens the experience of approaching the entry.

Clearly not every community has the possibilities of St. Peter's or Santa Fe. Can we express these concepts in a modest yet effective way? Figure 7 illustrates a very generous processional gathering space that directs people down a tree-lined path past a fountain toward a more expansive space directly before the portal. Figure 8 illustrates how this same gathering space invites people toward the

8. Ample spaces invite interaction.

entrance while at the same time it encourages visiting.

Each of these examples demonstrates gathering as a process involving both duration and space to be traversed. The church's gathering place is to be designed in such a way that it elicits from the participant an anticipation of what is to come and facilitates the gradual assimilation into the larger group.

Then the transformation of the many individuals into the body of Christ has begun.

Supporting Social Interaction

The human need for social interaction as part of coalescing into a larger group should be carefully considered. People who are comfortable with each other will participate in the worship rather than attend as spectators.

The early Christian church atrium, that "migrated forum," certainly suggests an animated centrum. All through the Middle Ages the plazas before churches were marketplaces, and in many European and Latin American cities they still are. (Figure 9) The flower or vegetable or lace markets in the open plazas in front of churches provide delight for the eye. Special events like the *Christkindlemarkt,* the Christmas market in Munich in which nativity scene figures, candles, ornaments and special festive candies and fruits are sold, attract crowds of bundled-up shoppers around the cathedral on cold December days. The open gathering place is not a barrier, but rather a link with the total life of the community.

The "business of faith," to use Aidan Kavanagh's words, is no less animated than an ancient Roman forum or a European plaza. Kavanagh likens the liturgical place to the ". . . Italian piazza, the Roman forum, the Yankee town green, Red Square moved under roof and used for the business of faith."[10] Our idea of a church interior often suggests a private quiet haven from the outside world. To the contrary, says Kavanagh, "It is a vigorous arena for conducting public business in which petitions are heard, contracts entered into, relationships witnessed, orations declaimed, initiations consummated, vows taken, authority exercised, laws promulgated, images venerated, values affirmed, banquets attended, votes cast, the dead waked, the Word deliberated, and parades cheered."[11]

9. The plazas around European churches provide a link between the church and the larger life of the community.

Marketplace Model

Church designers today, much like their forebears, should take into account what makes contemporary civic gathering places workable and inviting. Since the atrium was incorporated into church plans, the marketplace has played a role in the design of churches. Today's marketplace, the shopping mall, offers elements of interest and importance to contemporary designers of churches. But only the most desirable aspects of the civic gathering place are appropriate in designing for the people who are convening at the Lord's, not the merchants', invitation. The center of community action has migrated away from places of worship to the malls, and the scope of that action has sadly narrowed to the need (or even greed) of the consumer. Nevertheless, we still may learn something for church design from some contemporary examples of public areas for marketing.

In a book called *The New Religious Image of Urban America, The Shopping Mall as Ceremonial Center*, Ira Zepp, Jr., notes that shopping malls address the search for human interaction and what he describes as a need for order and orientation.[12] Zepp points out that mall floor plans with their central focal point of fountains and skylights often suggest the centered patterns of medieval rose windows, oriental mandalas or floor plans of cathedrals. The symmetry and central focus of Park City Mall in Lancaster, Pennsylvania, illustrates such a plan.[13] (Figure 10)

Zepp goes so far as to call malls a model of sacred space:

> Travelers, pilgrims, tourists and shoppers departing from a center find themselves renewed and strengthened as a result of the energy found there. Even if physically exhausted, their spirits are uplifted.[14]

Such a perception of malls may be no coincidence. James

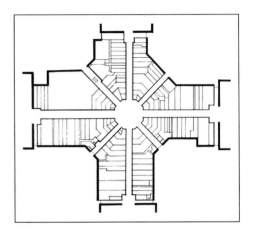

10. The symmetry and central focus of shopping malls sometimes look surprisingly like church plans.

Rouse, the "father" of modern malls and the designer of the newest "festival places" such as Harborplace in Baltimore, Faneuil Hall in Boston and Riverwalk in New Orleans, deliberately shaped his vision of the modern marketplace on values affirming the goodness of creation and the dignity of all human beings. This approach, which is certainly not that taken in most of our malls, reflects the public spaces created by the best town planners over the centuries.

Design Principles

What are some of the elements we might notice in malls and other public places that really invite and encourage interaction?

1. *Sufficient area.* In shopping malls, floor plans balloon out to accommodate fountains and seating areas around them. Huge atriums occupy the centers of museums and hotels (the word used for the gathering spaces in early Christian churches is now revived to mean the lobbies of such modern buildings). (Figure 11)

2. *Focal point.* There is a focal point of some kind. In a public park, the focus might be a monument, a fountain, an herb or rose garden, a pavillion, a panoramic

11. Open spaces in public buildings invite people to linger, to take in what is going on around them.

vista of a valley or a lake. A traffic pattern, in paths or planting arrangements, leads the visitor to the focal point. (Figure 12) Along the way one can expect to discover benches and perhaps tables.

3. *Paths.* There will usually be a "main" route, with other meandering paths offering quieter areas aside for sitting, reading or conversing.

4. *Human scale.* Even in spaces that soar overhead, objects and landscaping are designed to focus on the person. Furniture and landscaping establish a manageable scale in which people do not feel threatened by the architecture. (Figure 13) An atrium may tower many stories overhead, but cantilevered balconies extend out into the central space in a one-story scale. There may be a semicircular seating area, trees in pots or small-scale sculpture to establish an ambience that is human, even intimate,

12. Statues or fountains provide focal points in parks, orienting visitors.

13. Effective public buildings establish scale relationships.

within the vastness of the height
and breadth of the lobby.

5. *Ease of movement.* In successful public spaces, there is an
amplitude that does not allow people to be hurried or manipulated
into strictly defined patterns. (Figure 14) One occasionally discovers,
especially in outdoor places, paths
and paved walking areas that seem
to have no apparent geometric or
"designed" scheme but that nevertheless are inviting and comfortable. Such a layout, sometimes
referred to as a "cowpath" design,
reflects a scheme directly responsive
to the shape of what people actually
do intuitively in that space. Landscape architects quite wisely defer
to the customary behavior, having
before them the evidence of perhaps
generations of people who have
trodden a footpath across a meadow.

6. *Visual richness and variety.*
Attention is paid to the textures of
materials for floors and furniture.
Vast surfaces of brick or tile or

14. Satisfying public spaces do not manipulate human movement.

stone are softened by inlaid patterns, wood or light, living plants, the flowing water of fountains, fabric hangings. The whole environment is enlivened by color. (Figure 15)

Limitations of the Model

Although contemporary public gathering spaces have much that is positive to offer, one needs also to be aware of their limitations for churches. One such limitation may be scale. The mall is usually on a large scale, and the effects this has on design are significant. A more serious problem is that malls often express escapism and banality. An article in *Progressive Architecture* points out:

> Both of the inner-city shopping mall types—recycled buildings or new enclosed skylit galleries—reflect a strong element of escapism. The culture of consumption has always focused on this motif. But the tendency towards ersatz nostalgia on one hand, and controlled, filtered

15. A festive atmosphere prevails when there is visual richness and variety.

worlds on the other, pushes escapism over the edge into banality.[15]

We are more than capable of the same escapism in our churches: an insulated, protected, hothouse variety of Christian experience.

Shopping malls, unlike true civic spaces, are entirely introverted environments.[16] Cesar Pelli, principal architect in charge of the Courthouse Square in Columbus, Indiana, points out that a civic space "is a space designed to attract and be of use for many more occasions than shopping and at the same time is designed to draw people from the shopping center and bring them to the street itself."[17] The church, too, must both invite people inside and send them back to the larger world in which our mission will be carried out. A building and its environment can subvert the mission of the church by appearing either as a fortress or a fantasyland of escape from the larger world.

Specifics for Church Gathering

The gathering that is constitutive of the Christian assembly is undergirded by the following specific design concerns.

1. The size of the gathering area should be ample in relation to the size of the assembly. Some have suggested that the gathering area be at least one-third the area of the worship space.

2. The gathering space is to be related to other parts of the church, including the physical and climatic relationship to parking and entry. The gathering space must be on the main path to be successful.

3. The quality of the space will depend on:

- nature of the light (natural integrated with electric)

- nature of the materials (close-up as well as far-off; behavior over time)

- sound and noise control (from/to assembly, from outside)

- whether it must be used for overflow seating

- whether it includes kitchenette, storage, restrooms

- hospitality vs. security (at times other than worship)

- degree of adaptability, multi-use

- cost

Conclusion

The *Constitution on the Sacred Liturgy* states:

> In order that the liturgy may possess its full effectiveness, it is necessary that the faithful come to it with proper dispositions, that their minds be attuned to their voices, and that they cooperate with divine grace, lest they receive it in vain. Pastors must therefore realize that when the liturgy is celebrated something more is required than the mere observance

of the laws governing valid and lawful celebration; it is also their duty to ensure that the faithful take part fully aware of what they are doing, actively engaged in the rite, and enriched by its effects.[18]

We provide a gathering space that makes visible the significance of the coming together of the whole church for worship.

Vatican II initiated a reappraisal of how the church understands itself. As Mark Searle observes:

The recovery of the principle that the whole church celebrates the liturgy . . . represents first and foremost a recovery of the church's deepest conviction about the nature of the eucharist, a conviction which had never quite disappeared . . . but it had certainly been eclipsed by an understanding of the liturgy which focused almost exclusively on the role of the priest.[19]

The gathering for worship is itself constitutive of the identity of the Christian assembly.

Notes:

1. Dom Gregory Dix, *The Shape of the Liturgy* (London: Dacre Press, 1978), 142.

2. Mark Searle, "Collecting and Recollecting: The Mystery of the Gathered Church," *Assembly* (September 1984), 259.

3. As quoted by Marilyn Stokstad, *Medieval Art* (New York: Harper and Row, 1986), 317.

4. Richard Krautheimer, *Studies in Early Christian, Medieval and Renaissance Art* (New York: New York University Press, 1969), 15.

5. Roloff Beny and Peter Gunn, *The Churches of Rome* (New York: Simon and Schuster, 1981), 43.

6. Richard Krautheimer, *Rome, Profile of a City, 312–1308* (Princeton: Princeton University Press, 1980), 54.

7. Beny and Gunn, 43.

8. John Rupert Martin, *Baroque* (New York: Harper and Row, 1977), 151.

9. Barbara Schmich, "Entryways: Sacramental Spaces," *Assembly* (September 1984), 260–61.

10. Aidan Kavanagh, *Elements of Rite* (New York: Pueblo Publishing Company, Inc., 1982), 16.

11. Ibid.

12. Ira G. Zepp, Jr., *The New Religious Image of Urban America, The Shopping Mall as Ceremonial Center* (Westminster, Maryland: Christian Classics, Inc., 1986), 33.

13. Zepp, 45.

14. Zepp, 36.

15. Suzanne Stephens, "Introversion and the Urban Context," *Progressive Architecture* (December 1978), 53.

16. "New Directions for Downtown and Suburban Shopping Centers," *Architectural Record* (April 1974), 152.

17. Cesar Pelli, quoted in "New Directions for Downtown and Suburban Shopping Centers," 152.

18. *Constitution on the Sacred Liturgy*, 11.

19. Searle, 258.

CHAPTER 3

Entering and Going Forth

THE GATHERING OF the assembly is a coming together of many individuals who, despite their diversity, become one body of believers at worship. Passing through an entranceway affords entry into the building and signifies an assent to belonging to the community that is at home there. Entranceways ought to express the invitation to enter while they honor and celebrate the choice to cross the threshold into the life of the Christian community.

An Urban Image

The portal of the church has long been understood as the gateway to the heavenly city: This is the place where the New Jerusalem assembles itself. The psalms taught us these urban images:

> I rejoiced because they said to me,
> "We will go up to the house of the
>   LORD."
> And now we have set foot
>   within your gates, O Jerusalem—

Jerusalem, built as a city
  with compact unity.

To it the tribes go up,
  the tribes of the LORD,
According to the decree for Israel,
  to give thanks to the name of the
    LORD.
(Psalm 122:1–4)

Whenever public liturgies spill out into the streets and plazas, one can rightly say that the whole city becomes a church. The ancient processional liturgies of Jerusalem, Rome and Constantinople claimed the city as their sanctuary: Clergy and people processed through the streets to the sites commemorating the life and passion of Christ or to the shrines of martyrs.[1] John Chrysostom observed in the late fourth century that "the whole city has become a church for us."[2] In our own times we find that a papal visit turns vast open spaces and whole cities into a church. The expressways become a vehicular procession into the city as a gathering of the

assembly is already under way. Banners line the streets in festive welcome.

Our tradition has it that the bustle of city life is an image for God's encounter with people. Wherever we gather for worship, it will be a place filled with activity and energy and life. Such places are not important in and of themselves, but because of the things that are done there.

Threshold and Portal

For the solemn dedication of the temple in Jerusalem, Solomon convened all the elders and leaders of the tribes of Israel. In the midst of the whole assembly of Israel, Solomon prayed a long and wonderful prayer. He asked:

> Can it indeed be that God dwells among us on earth? If the heavens and the highest heavens cannot contain you, how much less this temple which I have built!
> (1 Kings 8:27)

Solomon acknowledged that the temple is for the assembly of the people to honor the Lord:

> May your eyes watch night and day over this temple, the place where you have decreed you shall be honored; may you heed the prayer which I, your servant, offer in this place. Listen to the petitions of your servant and of your people Israel which they offer in this place. Listen from your heavenly dwelling and grant pardon.
> (1 Kings 8:29–30)

A church deserves an entrance that implies to all who see it that the space on the other side is dedicated to certain deeds done regularly by the people who assemble there. A threshold marks the beginning of something new, arouses anticipation, invites the passerby to enter, to "come and see."

We know from the Hebrew Scriptures that the temple in Jerusalem included an opulent threshold. Not only were the pilgrims welcomed by small basins along the sides of the temple but also by a great basin of refreshing water resting on the backs of 12 bronze oxen within the courtyard surrounding the temple. Beyond the courtyard, an enormous porch thrust out toward them. Solomon hired a renowned bronze artisan, Hiram of Tyre, to cast bronze columns decorated with 200 bronze pomegranates each to flank a portal of stunning magnificence. These columns were so impressive they even had names, the one on the right called Jachin, the one on the left, Boaz (1 Kings 7:15–21).

The description of the portal of Solomon's temple calls to mind the triumphal arches of ancient Rome. Such splendid ceremonial entrances tell of the dignity and importance to whatever lies on the other side of them. The Arch of Titus in Rome (Figure 16) is certainly an ancestor for the stately entrance of the Chicago Public Library. (Figure 17) Architect Philip

16. Imperial arches express the solemn dignity of entering.

Johnson designed a grand arched portal that is 110 feet tall for his 1984 AT&T Corporate Headquarters building in New York. (Figure 18) Both Johnson and the architect of the Chicago Public Library back in the 1890s recognized that the entranceway sets the tone for our perception of what the building houses, an enticing gateway to what lies beyond.

17. Stately entrances
honor the activities
within the building.

18. Today as in ancient times, a dignified entry sets the tone for a building.

Historical Examples

The porch with its great bronze columns at the temple in Jerusalem thrust forward from the building as if to initiate the encounter with the pilgrims. In a similar manner the banistered porches of Victorian houses ballooned out from their facades extending an almost impulsive welcome. (Figure 19) The porches were often expansive enough to accommodate wicker rocking chairs and settees so that the entrance itself, as if to apologize for its overenthusiasm, provided a resting place, a transition between the well-kept yard and the household beyond the threshold.

As we saw in the last chapter, Bernini's seventeenth-century piazza (Figure 6) before St. Peter's in Rome embraces all in a gathering space that draws people toward the great facade and entry into the basilica. St. Peter's hardly provides a manageable model for the modest aspirations of most parishes. The

In the manner of a gate into a city or the simple entrance to a home, the doors of the church signal the point of access to the activity on the other side. The entryway becomes part of the hospitality extended by the occupants. The visitors' perception of the threshold precedes their reception by their hosts. Thus the treatment of the portal conveys a great deal about the eagerness, or perhaps reticence, with which visitors are anticipated and guided into the interior of the building. For those who come again and again the threshold must have the same power to welcome and to stir the imagination.

19. Domestic porches reach out in welcome.

20. The lines of the gathering spaces converge on the ceremonial entranceway.

21. Even if sometimes rather aggressive, entrances should be significant.

exaggeration of scale and pomp does, however, impress upon us the effectiveness of architecture that welcomes and shapes the entry in such a way that we know we are approaching and then passing through a significant passageway. (Figure 20)

A dramatic secular example of an important and compelling entrance is Michelangelo's design for the vestibule to the Laurentian Library in Florence. (Figure 21) In a shallow space the artist designed a staircase that pushes forward so audaciously that one almost backs off in the face of its cascading volumes. One critic describes the staircase as flowing "downward and outward so relentlessly that one wonders if we dare brave the current by mounting the steps."[3] Such an outpouring of eagerness seems perhaps overdone, yet the expressive indulgence on Michelangelo's part produced an architectural event long remembered once it has been experienced.

22. Older homes placed a high priority on entrances.

23. Hospitable porches are making a comeback.

Design Principles

Older homes often placed more emphasis on entryways than modern homes do (Figure 22), although ample and hospitable doors and porches (Figure 23) seem to be making a comeback over suburban designs in which half the front of the house is a garage. Many office buildings now seem to be incorporating plazas in front of their entries, which themselves are becoming more sculptural and alluring. (Figure 24)

The entry to a parking garage in Alexandria, Virginia, offers a fascinating example of a modern portal. (Figure 25) The design is contemporary but evokes the Gothic—including a rose window. It is such an astonishing surprise to find a parking garage whose entry suggests that something important lies on the other side. The customer feels honored—as if the building's owner values the sacred trust the customer places in the company.

What makes an effective entranceway for a house for the church? Certainly the portal must convey dignity and direction. Effective entrances reach out toward the visitor and guide all toward the primary passageway in such a way that the process engenders a sense of corporate progress, shared journey and a common destination. Flat sliding glass doors operated by sensor devices — as found in grocery stores — do not provide the

24. Corporate buildings are increasingly attentive to welcoming entries.

25. The architect and owner offer the public a memorable entry to a parking garage.

26. An entry gable thrusting through the roof line extends a wide gesture of welcome.

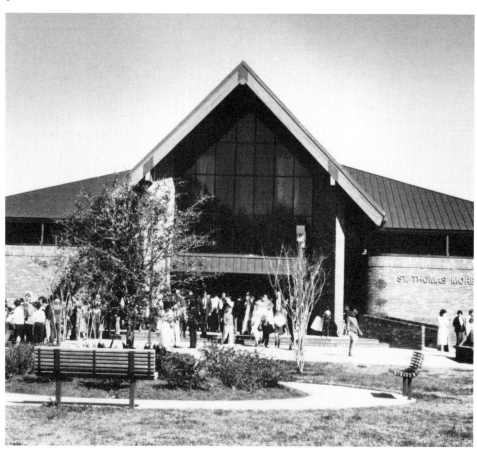

distinctiveness of threshold demanded by a house for the church. Nor do flat cantilevered porches—reminiscent of drive-in banks or gas stations—provide the dignity of a threshold to welcome the assembly.

Entranceways do not have to be ostentatious in order to shape the movement of people and communicate a sense of hospitality. Tall wings at an angle, flanking a portal and extending upward to a high pitched gable, can create a wide-open gesture of welcome. In the example illustrated in Figure 26, care has been taken that ramps for the handicapped are located in front of the flanged wings so that all who approach will find themselves within the architectural gesture of outreach and invitation.

An inclusive and hospitable entrance gesture expresses the mysterious image proclaimed by Jesus: "I am the gate of the sheepfold"

(John 10:7). A deliberately prominent portal that welcomes, yet does not intimidate, continues the image of Jesus: "Whoever enters through me will be safe." (John 10:9)

The task of gathering the many into one requires a single portal. Fire codes require several exits, but the designer who wants to shape people's experience of being drawn with others into the assembly will insist on a single, significant entranceway. Entrance signs with arrows may be helpful to visitors, but they betray a poverty of response to the meaning of gathering and entrance into the building and thus into the life of the community. The need for directional signs implies that one simply cannot immediately see where one should go. Such confusion is hardly desirable for an image of the spiritual journey—yet that journey is exactly what gathering spaces and entrances at their best model for us.

Beyond the Building

Significant entrances are not limited to architectural forms of the building itself. A creative design might incorporate existing full-grown trees on the site to function as a natural gateway, with the rest of the building in harmony with the natural forms, echoing the linear and vertical shapes of the trees. (Figure 27)

Another facet of summoning hospitality is sound—particularly in the form of bells. They summon to worship, ring out jubilation, mourn the dead. It is not an exaggeration to say bells speak. Pealing bells mimic the range of human speech and emotions. Bells ring with the voice of the body of Christ speaking words of welcome, of joy and of consolation. A medieval prayer for the consecration of a bell wonderfully describes how bells inspire faith and draw a holy people into the sacred precinct:

Wherever it reaches Christian ears, let there be increase of faith. Let it summon Christian folk to the bosom of mother church and there let them break out in a new song to the Lord with the music of the pipes, the sweetness of the tympany, the joy of the cymbals; as, in prayerful devotion, they invite into your holy place the very choirs of angels.[4]

The reverberation of bells, even the sight of their rocking back and forth with the clappers pounding, expresses the vitality of life itself in a way electronic speakers never could. Real bells affirm the principles of honesty and authenticity. They honor the variety of human experiences their peals observe and celebrate. Bells may soar overhead in a tower of their own or be incorporated into the structure of the building. Figure 28 illustrates one modern design in which the bells form part of the wall elevation of the church, not unlike the facades of mission churches of the old Southwest.

27. A creative entry design incorporates the natural environment.

28. Real bells can find a home in modern church designs.

29. The bells of mission churches remind us of their traditional role in the life of the community.

(Figure 29) The bells deserve to be visible. The sight of the bells along with their sound enhances the festive role of bells in the gathering and entrance of the assembly.

Going Forth

Portals express and extend a gesture of welcome for the gathering of the assembly. Portals serve also as an exit. Exiting has to do with mission. Leave-takings are dismissals to mission.

The dismissal rite with its commission to "go forth in peace to love and serve the Lord" is more a beginning than an adjournment. The Christian, nourished and refreshed, is sent forth from the "city" into the "city," into the world, to take up and to continue Christ's mission of service. A church's portal should invite and guide people into the place of assembly, then spill them forth, sent back into the larger world where the Lord is also to be encountered. The house for the church should not visually retreat from its neighborhood, its city, but rather vitally interact with its environment.

Connecting with the World Beyond

Architects of seventeenth-century baroque churches held this interaction with the immediate environment as a priority. Many of these churches front directly onto busy city streets. Taking a look at the interplay of protruding round forms and those that curve inward in one of these churches in Rome shows how the architect solved the problem of visually attracting people into the entrance passageway. The fat round portico of Pietro da Cortona's church of S. Maria della Pace pushes out from the front of the building, framed by concave wings on the upper story. More

widely spaced columns at the center of the portal invite entry into the church.[5] (Figure 30) The interplay of "spatial advance and retreat" also animates Bernini's church of S. Andrea al Quirinale. Again curving walls at the sides embrace a boldly aggressive porch surrounded by semicircular steps spilling down to the street.[6] (Figure 31) The curved steps slope downward, flowing outward toward the approaching visitor.

One last example of these baroque designs will serve to make an important point concerning the animation of portals. The facade of S. Carlo alle Quattro Fontane undulates before the visitor's eyes. The rhythm of Borromini's design advances and recedes on both stories in a serpentine manner, prominently thrusting toward the viewer at the center.[7] (Figure 32)

Each of these three architects utilized an interplay of projecting

and receding forms so that the entrance not only engages the viewer's eye but also enfolds as it thrusts out toward us. Such designs are images of vitality, of dialogue with the viewer. These entrances are much more than functional openings for access. They tantalize the viewer, sometimes even obstruct a pedestrian's path with steps that seem to overflow right onto the sidewalk, requiring the person to either step up onto them or walk around them. At any rate one cannot ignore these facades.

Design Specifics

To all these considerations of the task of the entranceway must be added the list of practicalities:

- circulation and ease of movement, handicap access, fire egress
- future adaptability
- climate compatibility

30. Baroque churches pushed right into the street.

31. Dramatic entry-ways enticed one to enter.

32. There is an energy in baroque portals that compels interaction with the viewer or passerby.

- site orientation and configuration (parking, etc.)
- sound/noise intrusion and control
- quality of materials, fire ratings, etc.
- scale, style
- context: architectural and environmental
- legal: zoning, easements, etc.

Conclusion

The baroque architectural vocabulary of classical columns and massive cornices is not appropriate for contemporary designs, but much might be gained from looking at and reflecting upon the dynamic interactions between building and viewer and between building and street achieved by these architects.

The idea was that an entrance should actively engage visitors, drawing them from the city of their busy lives into the city of the activity of God's people. This idea intrigues us with its symbolic possibilities. The entrance can vitally participate, as it has done in past ages, in unifying disparate individuals into a communal procession of the church gathered, coming and going. A well-designed entrance can express that being church requires response, that being church is an active endeavor.

Notes:

1. John F. Baldovin, "The City as Church, the Church as City," *Liturgy* (Fall 1983), 70.

2. Baldovin, 72.

3. H. W. Janson, *History of Art,* 2nd ed. (Englewood Cliffs, New Jersey: Prentice-Hall, Inc., 1982), 431.

4. From "Consecration of a Bell", *Roman Pontifical,* twelfth century. Cited by Mark Searle, *Assembly* (September 1981), 138.

5. John R. Martin, *Baroque* (New York: Harper and Row, 1977), 188.

6. Martin, 188–90.

7. Ibid.

CHAPTER 4

Initiation and Reconciliation

AT THE TIME when the cock crows, first let prayer be made over the water. Let the water be flowing in the font or poured over it. Let it be thus unless there is some necessity; if the necessity is permanent and urgent, use what water you can find. They shall take off their clothes. Baptize the little ones first. All those who can speak for themselves shall do so. As for those who cannot speak for themselves, their parents or someone from their family shall speak for them. Then baptize the men, and lastly the women, who shall have loosened all their hair, and laid down the gold and silver ornaments which they have on them. Let no one take any alien object down into the water.[1]

To "go down into the water" of baptism in the company of other men, women and children, naked, having left aside all adornments of this world, bears powerful testimony to the selfless surrender required of each person who would "put on the Lord Jesus Christ." The literal descent into the waters of death in order to be reborn into the life conferred by the Spirit is certainly an action capable of carrying the weight of the mystery of participation in the death and resurrection of Jesus. There is a great vulnerability in going naked into the unknown, of loosening one's hair and letting go all fetters, of leaving behind ornaments proclaiming the security of status and wealth.

The passage quoted above comes from a third-century document known as the *Apostolic Tradition,* a church order containing rules for Christian life and church discipline. Even today we read these early Christian instructions almost catching our breath at the stunning witness such a profession of faith represents. Our own minimalist experience of a few drops of water poured on an infant's head over a shallow bowl cannot begin to express a person's willingness to wade into the ambiguity of death emboldened by unconditional faith in the promise of life everlasting. We ask people to "remember your baptism" when sprinkling replaces the penitential rite at the beginning of Mass, yet for the most part people have no memorable experience of baptism to recall.

The experience of baptism as entry into the community and into the life of God imposes an additional layer of meaning for the architectural entry space. The entryway is not only the focus for the gathering of the assembly. The literal entry into the building ideally provides the ritual experiences of entry and reentry into the life of the community—baptism and reconciliation.

The Waters of Baptism

Baptism has been celebrated with so little symbolic power for so long that we have difficulty grasping that these rites define and identify the Christian assembly. The restored adult ritual sequence of baptism, confirmation and eucharist— celebrated in the Rite of Christian Initiation of Adults (RCIA) —is now the liturgical norm for entrance into the Roman Catholic communion.[2] A powerful new awareness of the commitment required to be church has taken hold in parishes that have embraced the RCIA. The whole community is renewed by the initiation of new members. Since the conversion process for those seeking full admission to the church occurs within the community of the faithful, "together with the catechumens, the faithful reflect upon the value of the paschal mystery, renew their own conversion, and by their example lead the catechumens to obey the Holy Spirit more generously."[3]

Something is lost when not enough water is used in baptism to convey anything of the notions of death or cleansing or rising to new life from the darkness of death. The baptismal traditions of the early Christian communities merit reflection in our search for ways to retrieve the richness and evocative power of baptism in the experience of modern Christians. We should look at our past for insight into what fonts might look like, what they have to do with the whole ritual life of the community, and where to put them.

Font Imagery

One writer has said that Christian baptism requires "a place for burial, birth and bath."[4] The funeral imagery of baptism is probably the most familiar as we recall the description in Romans 6:3–4:

> Are you not aware that we who were baptized into Christ Jesus were baptized into his death? Through baptism into his death we were buried with him, so that, just as Christ was raised from the dead by the glory of the Father, we too might live a new life.

This funeral imagery was expressed both in baptistry buildings that were derived from imperial mausoleums and therefore symbolized death, and by rectangular, coffin-shaped fonts. The hexagonal font represents another type of funeral image since the six-sided form alludes to the sixth day, the day on which Christ died.

Baptism is understood also as birth, and the font takes on the meaning of a womb. The gospel of John suggests the "born again" meaning of baptism in the dialogue between Nicodemus and Jesus (John 3:4–5):

> "How can a man be born again once he is old?" retorted Nicodemus. "Can he return to his mother's womb and be born over again?" Jesus replied: "I solemnly assure you, no one can enter into God's kingdom without being begotten of water and Spirit."

Round fonts are thought to express this birth or womb symbolism. Both tomb and womb symbolisms point to new life. One dies with Christ by going down into the waters of death, but then the person rises from those waters to life eternal with the resurrected Lord. Likewise, one is born in the waters of baptism into the new life of the resurrected Christ. Octagonal fonts beautifully convey the new life of the baptized Christian because they celebrate the eighth day as the day of the resurrection, as the day beyond time.

Abundant Water

The washing that is baptism requires a vessel that contains enough water and enough space to actually drench the baptismal candidate. Most early fonts were shallow pools. Except when baptisms took place in rivers or streams, the archeological evidence

33. A hexagonal font symbolizes baptism's funerary imagery: Christ died on the sixth day.

34. The baptized emerged from the waters of death into the octagonal resurrection space around the font: The eighth day is the day beyond time.

suggests that submersion was not the customary practice. Water was poured over the head of the catechumen who stood in a pool perhaps 18 inches deep. This type of baptism, technically called affusion, is what *Environment and Art in Catholic Worship* refers to as immersion:

> To speak of symbols and of sacramental signification is to indicate that immersion is the fuller and more appropriate symbolic action in baptism. New baptismal fonts, therefore, should be constructed to allow for the pouring of water over the entire body of a child or adult. Where fonts are not so constructed the use of a portable one is recommended. (76)

The mid-fifth-century octagonal baptistry in Grado (north of Venice) houses a shallow hexagonal font that speaks to us of neophytes going down into the waters of death and emerging into their new life, wet and shivering in the octagonal resurrection space surrounding the font. (Figures 33 and 34) Two

35. Modern fonts recall the shallow pools of early Christian times.

newly renovated churches, St. Charles Borromeo in London and the Nativity in Rome, include dramatic cruciform fonts that resonate with those pools of the early centuries. The baptized literally make their way through the paschal death of the cross by going down steps on one side and ascending the steps on the opposite side once they have been baptized. (Figure 35)

Other solutions include very unpretentious pools of simple materials such as the round brick font in Figure 36.

Although adult initiation is the ritual norm, the majority of baptisms in Roman Catholic parishes involve infants. The challenge is to design a font into which infants can be immersed, while at the same time accommodating the baptisim

36. Immersion fonts do not have to be extravagant.

of adults by the pouring of water over their entire bodies. Such designs usually include an elevated section for infant immersion with the water flowing from the upper basin into the larger pool below. The practical needs are felicitous: Such arrangements allow the sight and sound of the "living waters" to emphasize the life-giving sacrament. (Figure 37)

Other Rites

The baptismal waters link human experience with the death and resurrection of Jesus. Although adult baptism is now celebrated primarily at Easter and infant baptism more frequently during the year, the water of baptism comes into play in a variety of other circumstances throughout the year.

1. *Purification.* Since early Christian times, Christians have symbolically purified themselves upon entering a church. The holy water stoups at the doors of churches in all likelihood are a stripped-down version of the fountains in the courtyards of early churches. These provided for the refreshing washing of the hands and faces of the pilgrims.[5] A tiny container attached near the door only faintly recalls a memory of refreshment and cleansing. However, if the baptismal font of living water were the "holy water" font into which the faithful dipped their hands and made the sign of the cross, then a link might be made with the cleansing waters of baptism and continual cleansing, refreshment and renewal.

2. *Entrance blessing.* The blessing and sprinkling of the people with holy water is an alternative to the penitential rite at the beginning of the Sunday liturgy. The presider says, "Dear friends, this water will be used to remind us of our baptism." The prayer given in the

sacramentary then focuses on the refreshing and cleansing properties of the water of baptism:

> God our Father, your gift of water brings life and freshness to the earth; it washes away our sins and brings us eternal life. We ask you now to bless this water, and to give us your protection on this day which you have made your own. Renew the living spring of your life within us and protect us in spirit and body, that we may be free from sin and come into your presence to receive your gift of salvation.

The prayer for the blessing of water for the entrance rite during the Easter season summarizes in vivid images the life-giving and life-saving properties of water:

> Lord God almighty, hear the prayers of your people: we celebrate our creation and redemption. Hear our prayers and bless this water which gives fruitfulness to the fields, and refreshment and cleansing to us. You chose water to show your goodness when you led your people to freedom through the Red Sea and satisfied their thirst in the desert with

37. Elevated fonts for infant immersion facilitate "living water."

water from the rock. Water was the symbol used by the prophets to foretell your new covenant with humankind. You made the water of baptism holy by Christ's baptism in the Jordan: by it you give us a new birth and renew us in holiness. May this water remind us of our baptism and let us share the joy of all who have been baptized at Easter.

How much more powerful a sign such a blessing might be if the water recalling our baptism were carried with festivity from the font in which those Easter baptisms occurred. Texts such as these are the primary sources of reflection for those who set about the building and renovation of churches— as they are sources of formation for all the faithful.

3. *Funerals.* The rite at the entrance to the church provides for the blessing of the body with holy water. This rite is clearly envisioned as taking place near the parish font. At the end of mortal life the baptism into the death of Christ is recalled so that the promise of resurrection might also be remembered with joy:

> In the waters of baptism N. died with Christ and rose with him to new life. May he/she now share with him eternal glory.

If the body is not blessed with holy water at the entrance to the church, provision for this is made at the final commendation and farewell. The prayer is that the deceased be received into heaven in fulfillment of the baptismal covenant.

4. *Church dedication.* The *Rite for the Dedication of a Church* includes the sprinkling of the people: "The bishop blesses water and with it sprinkles the people, who are the spiritual temple, then the walls of the church, and finally the altar" (11). The prayer of blessing of the water (48) emphasizes that it is the unity of those who have gone through the waters of baptism and are heirs of Christ's covenant that constitute the church:

> God of mercy, you call every creature to the light of life and surround us with such great love that when we stray you continually lead us back to Christ our head. For you have established an inheritance of such mercy, that those sinners, who pass through water made sacred, die with Christ and rise restored as members of his body and heirs of his eternal covenant. Bless this water; sanctify it. As it is sprinkled upon us and throughout this church make it a sign of the saving waters of baptism, by which we become one in Christ, the temple of your Spirit. May all here today, and all those in days to come, who will celebrate your mysteries in this church, be united at last in the holy city of your peace.

The baptismal journey is the image of the whole Christian life. The evocative power of the baptismal journey permeates the community's consciousness when both the font with its flowing water and the lived experience of the RCIA become permanent in the lives of the faithful. Approaching the font of living water for personal blessings at the entry, the sprinkling rites at the beginning of Sunday liturgies, blessing the body at funerals, the rite for the dedication of churches, the many blessings the church celebrates with water—these recall again and again the baptismal "putting on of Christ" that is the life, the sustenance and the hope of Christians.

Principles

The baptismal font is thus the visual sign of something much larger than itself. The font with its living water reminds the faithful that they are made a people by water and the spirit, that they stand always ready to receive new members and be renewed, that baptism is the basis of who they are and who they want to be. Going down into the waters is the first thing

Christians do. It is the beginning of the Christian life whose earthly termination is blessed by that same baptismal water.

To be formative for the life of the community, the font must bear the weight of the mysteries celebrated there. It should have flowing "living" waters and be ample enough to allow for the pouring of water over an adult. As Aidan Kavanagh puts it, "Baptism into Christ demands enough water to die in."[6] The design of the font should also be appropriate for the immersion of infants.

The importance of the flowing water deserves special heed. It is the living water that is the reminder of baptism, not the font by itself. Richard Vosko observes:

> Water that has special meaning for the community is present to the community at all times. This means that water for baptism is not taken from the sink tap just before the rite begins. Rather, the water is a part of the environment for worship, constantly running . . . always refreshing the people who gather in the worship space.[7]

Placement

The baptismal font requires prominence to make apparent the priority of baptism in the community's life. The placement of the font is a very important decision. The natural place is as an obstacle in the entryway—as the only way in and the only way out. The font with its living waters should impinge on people's consciousness and assert realities of the Christian life.

There are several options for the location of the baptismal font within the assembly's view. They include the entranceway, in front of the assembly near the altar, a side location or a creative combination of the advantages of several of these possibilities.

1. *An entrance location.* (Figure 38) The role of the initiation rites within the life of the community makes a strong case for the placement of the font near the entranceway to the worship area. This incorporates the symbolic value of the font into the experience of the faithful. If the font is the only "holy water font" as people enter the church and bless themselves, if baptism is really perceived as a threshold event, if the bodies of the deceased are greeted and blessed at the entranceway, then the importance of threshold and newness and forgiveness and death and life will become tangible and memorable. Each time we enter the worship space we will confront the life-giving water that literally touches us week after week through the events and days of our lives. The cumulative effects of such familiarity must not be underestimated as a pilgrim people journeys the road of faith.

The disadvantage of this location is that the assembly might be obliged to turn around or stand at an angle to see the baptismal rites. Ade Bethune makes several cogent observations regarding this objection.[8] She points out that no one minds turning around at a wedding and that it is natural for people to face the sacred action, wherever it is taking place. Sometimes the entrance area will be large enough for everyone to leave their places and gather around the font. If visibility becomes a serious problem, then it would be appropriate for ministers to carry water in pitchers from the font to a temporary

38. An entry location for the font asserts baptism as the way into the life of the community.

39. An up front location of the font emphasizes baptism's relationship with eucharist.

40. An immersion font in front of the assembly facilitates visual access but sacrifices ongoing encounters with the font.

would locate the baptismal font near the focal place for the assembly. Because the assembly takes baptism so seriously, the proponents wish to ensure that all can see when the rites are celebrated. A forward position also emphasizes the relationship between baptism and eucharist. In the RCIA, the early Christian sequence of baptism, confirmation and eucharist is reclaimed. Baptism is admission to the eucharistic table, the sign of unity in the Lord.

The disadvantages include the possible visual competition between the font and the altar if, as it should be, the font is designed for the full celebration of immersion rites. There is also the forfeiture of a more personal and physical ongoing association with the font afforded by an entranceway location, an association capable of linking related experiences of community life.

basin near the front. Although such a solution probably precludes immersion and affusion, taking water from the font and even returning the water to the permanent font makes it clear that the water is significant and that it comes from a permanent source (not the faucet in the sacristy sink). It is the water of holy baptism.

2. *In front of the assembly.* (Figures 39 and 40) A second model

Compromises must be made with either an entrance or forward location of the font. As the celebration of baptism focuses more on the Easter Vigil as the single most appropriate time for the admission of new adult Christians, and as infant baptisms are celebrated less frequently during the year than in the past, the trade-offs should be carefully thought through when choosing a location for the baptistry.

3. *A side location.* (Figure 41) A third model is represented by placement of the font somewhat off the main threshold axis, yet not entirely at the front of the assembly. Depending on the arrangement of the seating of the assembly, there is the possibility of good sight lines with minimal turning in the pews. The problem of conflict of focus with the altar is avoided. Some creative solutions in renovation projects might include changing the whole axis of the worship space and utilizing the former apse as an elevated baptistry, thus assuring visibility and avoiding competition with the altar. (Figure 42)

The threshold experience may be lost with a side location, although this is not necessary if a

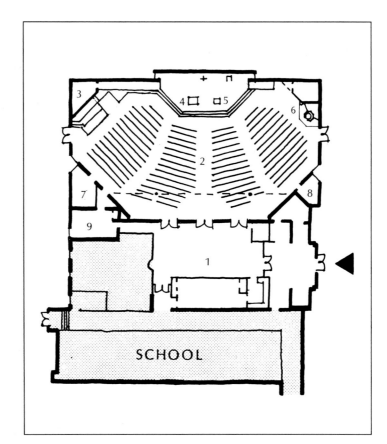

1 Gathering
2 Assembly
3 Music area
4 Altar
5 Ambo
6 Baptistry
7 Eucharistic reservation
8 Reconciliation chapel
9 Sacristy
10 Daily Mass chapel

41. A side location of the font offers good sight lines, but sacrifices the threshold experience.

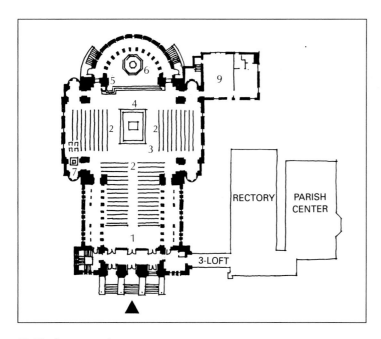

42. The former apse is a good possibility for an elevated font location in a renovation.

43. It is possible to have an entry location, good visibility, and axis of font and altar if some nontraditional seating arrangements are explored.

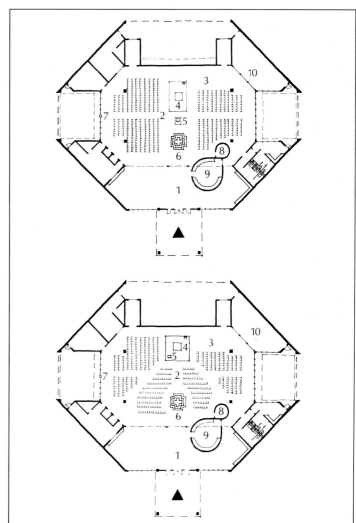

gathering space at the font invites people toward it and if the space can accommodate entrance processions.

4. *An innovative combination.* (Figure 43) Is it possible to combine an entrance experience of the baptismal water, proximity to the altar (a perception of the bond of font to table) and good visibility within the assembly without a conflict of focus with the altar? One possibility might be a large gathering space spiraling in a wide arc into the centrum or main worship area. The font might be located at the end of the curve and thus be near the altar yet part of the entrance.

What are some other possibilities? In a renovation, one might consider locating the font in the apse space of the familiar longitudinal axis and making the apse at the same time the main entry from a gathering space beyond. Frank Lloyd Wright's 1904 Unity Temple in Oak Park, Illinois, represents an early example of such a processional design. The congregation enters on either side of the pulpit, facing worshipers already seated. Not only do the worshipers encounter each other as they enter, but as Wright said, "This scheme gave the minister's flock to him to greet. Few could escape."[9] In order to design the ideal combination of an entry encounter with the font and simultaneously a visual proximity to the altar, a long axis with a center aisle may be lost—but processions do not have to follow straight lines and churches are not built just for brides. Movable seating would, of course, increase the possibilities for adjusting aisles for special circumstances.

Holy Oils

Canon law prescribes that pastors keep the holy oils "carefully in a fitting manner" (Canon 847). Hospitality suggests that the Christian community express its willingness to admit new members and to care for the sick by prominently displaying the oil of catechumens, chrism and oil of the sick. Though usually kept together, this is not necessary or even appropriate. One fitting place for the chrism is near the baptismal font, possibly in a lighted niche.[10] Vessels translucent enough to disclose the oil as oil, and large enough to contain a plenitude of oil, reveal God's generosity in attending to our needs.

Reconciliation: Rite of Reentry

At one time the rite of penance was called "second baptism," a reference to its development as a pastoral response to those who had publicly and gravely sinned after "first penance" or baptism. The shape of reentry in those early centuries was derived from baptism's catechumenal journey. The sinner was enrolled in the order of penitents and embarked upon a rigorous program of penitential prayer, fasting and almsgiving. Depending upon the gravity of the sin, this could last for a number of years. The assembly supported the penitents by their prayers until the time of reconciliation and readmission to the community. When postbaptismal penance was a once-in-a-lifetime possibility, it was seen as an arduous journey of transformation accomplished within the context of the community.

Christ's paschal mystery reconciled us to God. We experience this first in baptism. As the Introduction to the *Rite of Penance* puts it, the victory of Christ over sin

> is first brought to light in baptism where our fallen nature is crucified with Christ so that the body of sin may be destroyed and we may no longer be slaves to sin, but rise with Christ and live for God. For this reason the church proclaims its faith in

"the one baptism for the forgiveness of sins." (2)

The primary sacraments of reconciliation remain baptism and eucharist.

> In the sacrifice of the Mass the passion of Christ is made present; his body given for us and his blood shed for the forgiveness of sins are offered to God again by the church for the salvation of the world. In the eucharist Christ is present and is offered as "the sacrifice which has made our peace" with God and in order that "we may be brought together in unity" by the Holy Spirit. (Introduction to the *Rite of Penance*, 2)

For each of these sacraments of reconciliation there is a visual sign that immediately suggests the fuller implications of the actions to which they allude—the font with its waters of passage from death to life and the table around which we gather to eat the bread and drink the cup of the new covenant for the forgiveness of sins.

Rite of Penance

The rite of penance, unlike the sacraments of baptism and eucharist, has no tangible object that effectively discloses the extent of its meaning. The "sign" of the sacrament of reconciliation is the laying on of hands, and no object or piece of furniture is needed. Until recently a visual sign of reconciliation was the confessional box. Since the revision of the rite in 1973, the reconciliation chapel has been such a sign. This association is problematic, for the reconciliation room defines a private encounter with a confessor, a one-to-one experience that seems not to take into account the ecclesial nature of the celebration as described in the Introduction to the rite.

When that Introduction speaks of the sacrament of penance, it stresses the communal nature of the sacrament on the part of a church "which includes within itself sinners and is at the same time holy and always in need of purification" (3). The Introduction makes clear that reconciliation is both with God and with the church:

> In the sacrament of penance the faithful "obtain from the mercy of God pardon for their sins against him; at the same time they are reconciled with the church which they wounded by their sins and which works for their conversion by charity, example, and prayer."
>
> "By the hidden and loving mystery of God's design we are joined together in the bonds of supernatural solidarity, so much so that the sin of one harms the others just as the holiness of one benefits the others." Penance always entails reconciliation with our brothers and sisters who are always harmed by our sins. (4, 5)

The celebration of reconciliation should disclose the social and communal dimensions of personal sin and challenge the community to mutual support of the sinner in the conversion process. Such support would be for the church's mission of building the reign of God.

Options for the Rite of Penance

The "Rite for the Reconciliation of Individual Penitents," the first of three options in the revised rites, is the familiar rite of private confession. The second option is "Reconciliation of Several Penitents with Individual Confession and Absolution," a communal structure only to the extent that it is a gathering of individual penitents for a word service followed by individual confession and absolution. The third option for the "Reconciliation of Penitents with General Confession and Absolution" comes laden with many restrictions. Ralph Kiefer summarizes:

> In a word, while the *Ordo Poenitentiae (Rite of Penance)* asserts with considerable vigor that reconciliation is corporate and ecclesial, it fails to provide any effective means of full ecclesial and corporate celebration of reconciliation. The role of the assembly remains a dispensable addendum. While other documents effectively describe (and effectively make ritual provision for it) the role of the assembly as co-celebrants of baptism and the eucharist, this role is effectively denied in the ritual provisions of the *Ordo Poenitentiae*.[11]

Because the rite for individual penitents does not express the stated ecclesial nature of reconciliation, the designer is faced with a dilemma in attempting to provide a space. What will support the ritual action and enable it to shape people's experience and perceptions? If the architect simply includes an appropriately hospitable "reconciliation chapel" in a convenient location, then the most that can be said is that a minimal concession has been made to the rubrical demands for anonymous or face-to-face options for individual penitents.

Somehow a way must be found to lead people from a private experience of penance and reconciliation to the communal one whose nature the Introduction to the rite presumes and whose experience is somewhat alluded to in the gathering for the word service of the second rite.

Principles

Sin, penance and reconciliation are mysteries. Reconciliation is a process, a journey requiring experiences of conversion, change, growth, dying and rising. How can we make visible that one of the most important aspects of Christian life is this reconciliation in Christ?

The tradition of the church from its beginning has been to tie the fundamental elements of Christian identity to a rite and to a place: baptism and the font of living waters, eucharist and the altar table. A reconciliation chapel can-

not carry such a burden. It can only refer to what people know. If their encounters with reconciliation are limited to private account keeping with the Lord, a reconciliation chapel will be a minor priority, fitted in wherever there might be a place not reserved for something more important. From such a viewpoint, reconciliation is not a major community activity demanding honor of place.

Yet reconciliation is a *prime* concern of the Christian community. We let go of our human frailty and weakness in the death of baptism so that the Lord may lift us up. As the familiar words at the preparation of the eucharistic gifts petition, "By the mystery of this water and wine may we come to share in the divinity of Christ, who humbled himself to share in our humanity." Lives lived in imitation of Christ's are affirmed each time we come to the table and offer our

lives, with Christ, whose death has reconciled us to God.

The Place of Reconciliation

For now, the visible reminder of reconciliation remains the reconciliation room. To evoke more effectively the ecclesial dimension of the rite as described in the Introduction to the *Rite of Penance,* while at the same time observing the rubrical norms, some suggestions are made here.

1. *As a sign of unity and reentry; near the baptistry.* The reconciliation room should have a place near the baptistry. The two should have a clear relationship as threshold experiences of conversion leading to the eucharistic table. This relation gives clear priority to the font from which penance takes its meaning. If the signs of entry and reentry are seen as inseparable from each other, then we can begin to identify the reconciliation that is baptism

with the baptismal cleansing that is the essence of the process of reconciliation. The presence of the flowing water of the font would encourage the intuitive gesture of blessing oneself with baptismal water when emerging from the celebration of the rite of reconciliation, thus tangibly signifying what few might otherwise consciously articulate.

2. *As a sign of unity: open to the eucharistic space.* As noted in the Introduction to the *Rite of Penance*, reconciliation is with God and with the church. Because our primary sign of unity is the gathering at the eucharistic table, the reconciliation room should ideally open into the eucharistic space. It is inappropriate to tuck it away in some unobtrusive place out of sight of the assembly. The reconciliation room can assert a strong symbolic presence if the place signaling the celebration of reentry and reunion has an obvious

and prominent location linking the threshold of entry to the eucharistic table. (Figure 43) A more theologically consistent placement of the reconciliation room can help encourage the community's corporate endeavors at understanding reconciliation as a major tenet of the faith, a primary identification of the Christian community and a way of life characterized as a journey from death to life.

A relationship between the reconciliation room, the baptistry and the eucharist is a beginning step toward an expression of the ecclesial spirit of the sacrament of reconciliation.

Conclusion

This chapter considers the rites of entry and reentry into the Christian community, baptism and reconciliation. The entire process of baptism, beginning with entry into the catechumenate and culminating in

reception at the eucharistic table, is seen as the embracing of a life of conversion. The entire community becomes involved in the incorporation of new members. The faithful renew their own conversion while journeying with the catechumens.

The baptismal journey is the image of the whole Christian life. A consideration of how often baptismal water is used in blessings and other rites suggests the permanent, visible and prominent presence of this water in the midst of the assembly.

Notes:

1. *Hippolytus: A Text for Students,* trans. Geoffrey J. Cumming (Nottingham: Grove Books, 1976), 18.

2. Aidan Kavanagh, *The Shape of Baptism: The Rite of Christian Initiation* (New York: Pueblo Publishing Company, Inc., 1978), 109, 126.

3. *Rite of Christian Initiation of Adults,* 4.

4. See S. Anita Stauffer, "A Place for Burial, Birth and Bath," *Liturgy* 5:4 (1986), 51–57. This is an excellent summary of the history of the early Christian baptismal fonts and their meanings. I am indebted to Stauffer for the conciseness and accessibility of her account. See also James Notebaart, "The Font and the Assembly," *Liturgy* 5:4 (1986), 59–65.

5. Joseph A. Jungmann, *The Mass of the Roman Rite,* II (New York: Benziger Brothers, Inc., 1955), 77.

6. Kavanagh, 179.

7. Richard S. Vosko, "The Christian Water Bath," *Liturgy* (January 1980), 29.

8. Ade Bethune, "The Primacy of the Font," *Sacred Signs* (Michaelmas, 1980), 2–3.

9. See John D. Wright letter in *Environment and Art Letter,* 1:9 (November 1988), 4. For the Frank Lloyd Wright quote, see Roger Kennedy, *American Churches* (New York: The Crossroad Publishing Co., 1982), 32.

10. Peter Mazar suggests other possible locations for the oils in *Liturgy 80* (July 1988), 8–10.

11. Ralph Kiefer, "The *Ordo Poenitentiae:* Revised Doctrine and Unrevised Ritual," *Hosanna* (1982), 20.

CHAPTER **5**

Eucharist

THE PIES HAD been baked the day before, pumpkin, apple, and mince; as we ate them, we could look out the window and see the cornfield where the pumpkins grew, the trees from which the apples were picked. . . . The bread had been baked that morning, heating up the oven for the meat, and as my aunt hurried by I could smell in her apron the freshest of all odors with which the human nose is honored—bread straight from the oven. . . .

All families had their special Christmas food. Ours was called Dutch Bread, made from a dough halfway between bread and cake, stuffed with citron and every sort of nut from the farm—hazel, black walnut, hickory, butternut. . . . The last deed before eating was grinding the coffee beans in the little mill, adding that exotic odor to the more native ones of goose and spiced pumpkin pie. Then all would sit at the table and my uncle would ask the grace, sometimes in German, but later, for the benefit of us ignorant children, in English:

Come, Lord Jesus, be our guest,
Share this food that you have
 blessed.

The first act of dedication on such a Christmas was to the occasion which had begun it, thanks to the child of a pastoral couple who no doubt knew a good deal about rainfall and grass and the fattening of animals. The second act of dedication was to the ceremony of eating. My aunt kept a turmoil of food circulating, and to refuse any of it was somehow to violate the elevated nature of the day.[1]

The gathering of the family, the special preparation of the fruits and grains of the earth, the anticipation, the dedication to the event celebrated, the ceremony of eating so wonderfully evoked in Paul Engle's remembrance of past Christmases with his family, describe the key elements of the eucharistic feast celebrated by Christians. Eucharist is an activity that engages the entire faithful in gathering, praising, remembering, offering, eating and drinking. In the words of the *Constitution on the Sacred Liturgy:* "All who are made children of God by faith and baptism should come together to praise God in the midst of his church, to take part in the sacrifice, and to eat the Lord's Supper." (10)

How do we recognize and experience that it is all God's people, by faith and baptism, who gather to take part in the sacrifice? That eucharist is a sign of unity with the Lord and this people? Designing a place for the celebration of eucharist requires attention to some issues with implications that impinge directly on design concepts.

Assembly as the Primary Symbol

The American Bishops' document *Environment and Art in Catholic Worship* (EACW) boldly says that "among the symbols with which liturgy deals, none is more important than this assembly of believers" (28). The gathered people are the most important symbol with which liturgy deals. "The most powerful experience of the sacred is found in the celebration and the persons celebrating; that is, it is found in the action of the assembly: the living words, the living gestures, the living sacrifice, the living meal." (EACW, 29). This is not a new idea, but one whose authenticity in the tradition is revealed by the design of early Christian churches as open gathering spaces that "allowed the whole assembly to be part of the action" (EACW, 29).

Priesthood of the Faithful

Perhaps the best way to understand the significance of the assembly as the primary liturgical symbol is to look at some of the ways in which the people have been described. This would include such ideas as the Mystical Body of Christ, the "priesthood of all believers," the assembly as the "people of God."

These designations make demands on the shape of worship spaces, demands that are quite different from those made by understandings of church based on other ecclesial models.

Before Vatican II, most Catholics had an understanding that priests performed holy actions for the benefit of the rest of the assembly. The congregation watched the rites but often were more involved in their own personal devotions than in participating in the liturgy celebrated in Latin. The higher elevation of the altar area as well as its distance from the people, fenced off by the altar railing, effectively reserved the "sanctuary" for the priest and the ritual he performed. The rank of the priest and the greater importance of the place from which he officiated was clearly distinguished from that of the laity and the space they occupied. (Figure 44)

A theaterlike design in which a proscenium arch sets off a performance stage is not suitable for today's liturgy. Instead, led by the presider, the assembly of believers joins with Christ in worship of the Father. It is not only the priest who makes the offering, but all the people. (Figure 45) The story of how the church arrived at this renewed view of the nature of her worship is a story primarily of biblical and theological reflection.

Background

The raging destruction and hatred during World War II prompted Pope Pius XII to reflect in those turbulent times on the unity of the church and our union in it with Christ. He promulgated an encyclical letter, *The Mystical Body of Christ,* in June of 1943.[2] In the opening sentence he identified the church as the Mystical Body of Christ. He pointed out that the celebration of

44. The separation of the priest from the people cannot express our present understanding of the assembly.

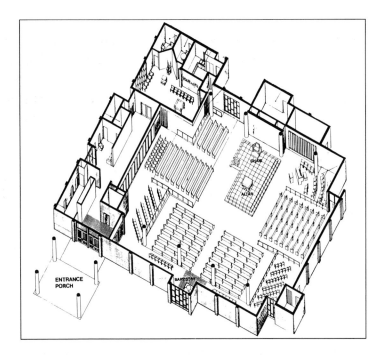

45. The seating arrangement becomes critical for the experience of the entire assembly offering eucharist.

eucharist is a sign of our unity among ourselves and with Christ. This unity is experienced as the faithful, united with the priest in prayer and desire, offer an acceptable sacrifice for the needs of the whole church.[3]

Thus some 20 years before Vatican II, Pius XII had already begun to voice in an official way a renewed understanding of the relationship of the people to the act of worship. Pius XII further refined his initial thoughts of the 1943 encyclical in a major encyclical on the liturgy in 1947. In this letter, *Mediator Dei*, he quotes early doctors of the church as well as the seventeenth-century scholar Robert Bellarmine in favor of the position that all the faithful participate in the offering of Christ at eucharist.[4] In further support he quotes the text of the eucharistic liturgy itself.[5] For example, he recalls the prayer after the offering of the bread and wine in which the presider turns to the people and says, "Pray that our sacrifice may be acceptable to God, the almighty Father." Other familiar plural prayers include the text of Eucharistic Prayer I, "Father, accept this offering from your whole family."

There is an inescapable implication of these prayers that the faithful, with the priest, make the offering. The faithful share in the priesthood of Christ by virtue of their baptism into the Mystical Body of Christ, and Pius XII said this in no uncertain terms.[6]

In 1964, this wisdom of Pius XII was incorporated into the *Dogmatic Constitution on the Church (Lumen Gentium)*. Chapter 2, entitled "The

People of God," sets forth in some detail the participation by baptized believers in the priesthood, prophetic office and apostolic mission of Jesus. Here again the assertion is made that the faithful offer the divine victim to God, and they offer themselves, their lives. This describes the role of the priesthood of the laity.[7]

Participatory Role

The 1975 *General Instruction of the Roman Missal* draws the practical implications of this understanding for the participatory role of the assembly. The text goes so far as to say that the royal priesthood of believers is a "reality of which much should be made" (5).

This Roman document includes two extremely provocative ideas. The first is that the role of the ordained priest is to bring to completion in union with Christ the people's spiritual sacrifice to God. The focus is thereby shifted to the offering of the whole church. To perceive eucharist as the offering of all believers in concert is to see the faithful exercising their appropriate priesthood. As the document instructs, "In this way greater attention will be given to some aspects of the eucharistic celebration that have sometimes been neglected in the course of time" (5). Certainly the spatial arrangement for the celebration of liturgy would have to be rethought in this light.

The second important insight in the *General Instruction* in its consideration of the priesthood of believers is that the people are gathered by the Lord. The role of priesthood is not one arbitrarily appropriated by the people as some new innovation. It is, in fact, conferred by Christ, who redeemed the people of God by his death and resurrection and now calls them to give thanks "for the mystery of salvation by offering his sacrifice" (5).

To share in Christ's priesthood is new language for many people. For such a long time the liturgy was understood as an activity carried out by the ordained clergy on behalf of the church. In baptism, however, all the faithful are consecrated into a holy priesthood. Even those who are not ordained to the ministerial priesthood share in the priesthood of Christ. "The faithful, on their part, in virtue of their royal priesthood, join in the offering of the eucharist."[8]

In order for the faithful to fully participate in the offering of the eucharistic sacrifice, they must perceive that they are more than spectators at a solemn presentation performed for their benefit. The offering of praise, the offering of petitions spoken on their behalf, the offering of themselves along with Christ whose death reconciled them to himself, must take place *among*, not in front of, the people.

The eucharistic table, sign of the unity of Christ present among his people, belongs in their midst. The configuration of people, presider and altar must reveal that the action of offering eucharist is one in which the entire assembly participates. In effect all the faithful offer lives of sacrifice with Christ, and all approach to eat and drink together in assent to the Lord's invitation to become one with him.

The Quest for the Holy

Given the ambiguities of the modern world, many people feel bereft of the sacred, the holy, the numinous. How can we meet the need for the holy in a culture that revels in all that is disposable?

Christian theology asserts the holiness of all creation. Such a stance questions a rigid distinction between the so-called sacred and profane. At the same time, one must not adopt a naive incarnationalism that would ignore the presence of evil and all its consequences in the world. With great insight Monika Hellwig has pondered this apparent contradiction. She notes that in the Christian experience of living between the already and the not yet, there is the eschatological tension between the assertion of the holiness of all creation and the realization that creation can betray us.

> In that process we must at the same time create holy places and maintain that every place is holy. We must simultaneously maintain the sense of the sacred and insist that there is not really any such distinction as that envisioned by a vocabulary of sacred and profane.[9]

If the locus of the holy is human beings and their activity, then it becomes clear that no one place is more sacred (or secular) than any other. No architecture of itself is holy just because it displays pointed arches or a vaulted roof or a steeple or stained glass or any other reference to forms we ordinarily associate with churches as "sacred places." Yet, a holy people doing holy actions consecrates a place.

Such a place should command profound respect for what happens in that precinct. One reason that pre–Vatican II churches seemed like such holy places, in spite of being full of production-line plaster statues, was that there was no question about the reverence held before all those things and what they represented. The way in which they were arranged, cared for and dealt with expressed a perception of their extraordinary roles in somehow referring to realities larger than the everyday.

Broken, needy people seek a place to come together and be nourished, refreshed and healed.

But we do not recognize the sacred in precincts of public ritual, for in our culture "the sense of the sacred is something private, personal, interior, and intimate; the sacred is closely attached to the self, not to rituals celebrated and shared in public."[10]

Perceiving the Holy Place

Many modern churches have cleared out all the "pious" statues and decorations that addressed the private devotional lives of the faithful but have not worked to prepare a liturgy that mediates the sacred. Some people are truly bereft of what they understood as holy places; others have little sense for what that would mean. Most still watch a familiar performance in which no one seems to be concerned about its holiness. The environment may be "stripped" or full of clutter, but the experience does not lead anywhere. It is no wonder people feel deprived.

A precinct for the mediation of the holy has always been understood as a specially designated place. Even the early Christian "house churches," which appeared undistinguished on the exterior, revealed special arrangement on the inside to enhance and support the ritual actions. The third-century house church at Dura Europos is an example. Walls were knocked out to enlarge the gathering space, a place was designated for the presider and a baptistry was installed. Specific efforts made that house a place capable of supporting the sacred rites celebrated there.[11]

We need an environment that grants priority to our common ritual. This seems to be what EACW calls for in several passages.

> The experience of mystery which liturgy offers is found in its God-consciousness and God-centeredness. This involves a certain benefi-cial tension with the demands of hospitality, requiring a manner and an environment which invite contemplation (seeing beyond the face of the person or the thing, a sense of the holy, the numinous, mystery). A simple and attractive beauty in everything that is used or done in liturgy is the most effective invitation to this kind of experience. One should be able to sense something special (and nothing trivial) in everything that is seen and heard, touched and smelled, and tasted in liturgy. (12)

> An action like liturgy, therefore, has special significance as a means of relating to God, or responding to God's relating to us. . . . Our response must be one of depth and totality, of authenticity, genuineness, and care with respect to everything we use and do in liturgical celebration. (13)

A response of totality, of authenticity, demands an environment with clarity of purpose. This is difficult to convey in a place designed to serve a half dozen or so different purposes. The invitation to contemplation and reflection legitimately requires a space with a character all its own, one the worshipers can depend on.

Materials and Objects

In the midst of fragmentation, we need images of wholeness to reaffirm life's own holiness and unity. The assembly, the body of Christ, is such an image. The environment with which it surrounds itself will reveal how it thinks of itself.

There is no dividing line marking some materials as sacred and some as secular. The distinction we must make has to do with how materials are used. For example, many uses of plastic are not suitable. An obvious instance would be the use of plastic to imitate natural materials such as wood. A "wood grain" plastic laminate altar stands in contradiction to the integrity of what is done at that table. Honesty and truthfulness is demanded of the table itself. However, in the proper setting, well-designed Plexiglas or acrylic furniture may be effective and desirable. An example is the furniture for the chapel in the Jesuit Renewal Center in Milford, Ohio. This acrylic furniture, designed by William Schickel and Associates, was selected by *Industrial Design* for the *1969 Design Review* and was included in a special exhibition in Chicago at the Museum of Science and Industry in 1970. The choice of any material must involve what the design will look like, how long the materials will last, and the relationship to other objects and the overall environment. The design for using the materials should have an integrity because it has respected the properties of the materials and therefore expresses their true nature.

The choice, arrangement and treatment of the material elements either devalue or reverence the mysteries we celebrate at liturgy. The way in which all the objects (furniture, vessels, flowers, walls, lighting, etc.) are made and assembled and used reveals how the assembly values itself and its worship.

Response

Given these goals—the assembly itself as the chief liturgical symbol, the exercise of the priesthood of the faithful as the way in which all the baptized participate in the offering of eucharist, a desire for a place people perceive as a holy precinct —what choices can we make? What would an ideal new church be like? What can we do with an old church that we love, even though at present it does not really allow for the liturgy to be celebrated as the church intends? These are the questions to be addressed now.

The Arrangement of the Assembly

The arrangement of pews or chairs in relationship to the altar provides instant insight into how a community perceives itself as church. The choice of a seating arrangement reveals the model that in all likelihood informs the whole life of the community.

The goal for designers is to provide the best possible environment for the assembly to celebrate the rites. Embracing this challenge frees designers from the tyranny of the aesthetic appeal of past ages and thus allows for freedom from the shaping power of those forms that no longer express what the Christian community proclaims to itself and all others. The simple truth is that the liturgy as reformed following Vatican II cannot be celebrated in the settings of the previous rites. Most clearly, the theater-style arrangement of the assembly makes it impossible to carry out the present liturgy.

Principles

The church earnestly desires that all the faithful be led to that full, conscious, and active participation in liturgical celebrations called for by the very nature of the liturgy. Such participation by the Christian people as "a chosen race, a royal priesthood, a holy nation, God's own people" is their right and duty by reason of their baptism. (*Constitution on the Sacred Liturgy,* 14)

To enable this experience by the whole community at eucharist requires a subordination of the room and its arrangement to the shape of the rite. That is the simple truth and starting point. Respect for its architectural and artistic merit or sentimental attachment to an old structure should not preclude creative ways to allow the building to yield new and life-giving possibilities. Likewise, designs for new churches must make clear that the words we hear describe what we are experiencing:

> *We, your people and your ministers,* recall his passion, his resurrection from the dead, and his ascension into glory; and from the many gifts you have given us *we offer* to you, God of glory and majesty, this holy and perfect sacrifice: the bread of life and the cup of eternal salvation. (From *Eucharistic Prayer I,* emphasis added.)

Placement

Most simply stated, the altar must be located *among* the people in order for the entire assembly to participate in the eucharistic prayer. There are numerous ways in which this can be achieved, ranging from the "fan" shapes and circular arrangements to Greek cross designs, reorientations of older longitudinal plans and even "monastic choir" arrangements.

The detachment of the altar platform from a back wall dramatically frees the altar from an implied sanctuary distinct from the area occupied by the assembly. A free-standing platform works particularly well in a renovation of a Gothic or Romanesque or Renaissance revival church. In these churches, a platform, thrust forward from the old apse and maintaining its elevation, often fails because it brings into the larger area all the old connotations of a space that is more important than and separate from the assembly's. The renovated Benedictine Sisters' chapel in St. Joseph, Minnesota, represents an especially successful solution by placing the altar on an island platform in the transept. (Figure 46)

46. An "island" platform for the altar brings it into the midst of the people, making the whole of a lovely old church the "sanctuary."

Examples

Light of the World Catholic Church in Littleton, Colorado, represents a deliberate revival of the early Christian basilica plan. (Figure 47) Here, as in old St. Peter's (Figure 2), there is a longitudinal orientation of the worship space preceded by an atrium or courtyard. In the modern building, a daily Mass chapel and a foyer separate the two. The baptistry is located just inside the foyer entrance into the completely adaptable worship space.

The church of Our Lady of Mount Carmel in Newport News, Virginia, also derives from the early Christian longitudinal basilica.

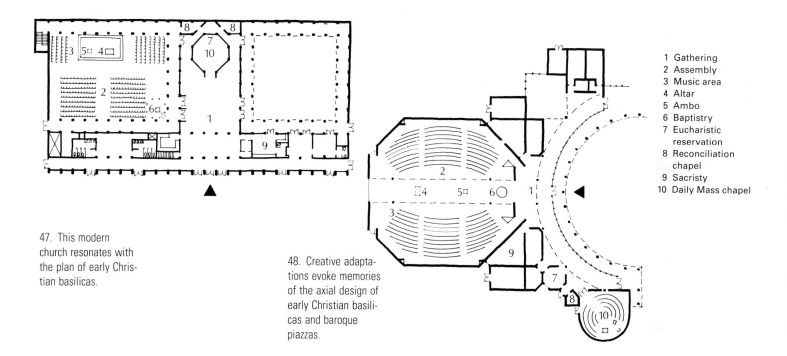

47. This modern church resonates with the plan of early Christian basilicas.

48. Creative adaptations evoke memories of the axial design of early Christian basilicas and baroque piazzas.

1 Gathering
2 Assembly
3 Music area
4 Altar
5 Ambo
6 Baptistry
7 Eucharistic reservation
8 Reconciliation chapel
9 Sacristy
10 Daily Mass chapel

(Figure 48) It includes an oval colonnaded atrium preceding the building—recalling Bernini's piazza in front of the baroque St. Peter's (Figure 6)—to provide an elegant gathering space. Inside a quite unexpected move has been made. Along the length of the rectangular space the seating follows a monastic (or antiphonal) arrangement with the people facing each other across the center aisle. The altar and ambo are located at opposite ends of the center aisle.

This arrangement for seating seems to be gaining in appeal for parish churches, appearing not only in new buildings, such as the one in Newport News, but also in some renovations. The Madonna della Strada chapel at Loyola University in Chicago demonstrates a harmonious adaptation of an older building to new liturgical norms.

49. An older building elegantly embraces a new arrangement of the assembly.

modated in a gracious and quiet elegance. (Figure 49)

The St. Thomas More student chapel in Norman, Oklahoma, offers a less formal, yet effective, appropriation of the monastic arrangement within a long, rectangular space. (Figure 50)

A combination of antiphonal seating and the conventional orientation gathers worshipers around altar and ambo in the renovated sanctuary at St. Bernard Church in Omaha, Nebraska. The altar stands on a round platform in front of its earlier position in the apse. The ambo is located on the longitudinal axis down the old center aisle, with seating on each side facing the center. Chairs fill the rest of the nave facing the altar in the traditional manner. (Figure 51)

Dealing with Older Churches

The renovation of older churches presents special challenges. In some

The features of the original building—including its elaborate and monumental image of the enthroned Virgin occupying the entire apse wall—have been accom-

cases one finds structures that are extremely long and narrow, imposing limitations on what can be done to them. A different set of circumstances accompanies renovation projects that begin as a response to some pressing maintenance problem in an old structure. The decision then gets made to do some liturgical renovation while everything is going to be torn up anyway. These projects often begin with severe budget limitations as the maintenance problem has the greater priority. Whatever the nature of the limitations though, creative solutions can usher new life and meaning into old buildings.

Examples

A particularly effective renovation of a nineteenth-century rural wooden church was accomplished at St. Amant, Louisiana, by vastly simplifying the old apse, thrusting the altar platform far forward and setting the pews in the long nave at

50. The "monastic" seating plan effectively gathers students in a university church.

a nine-degree angle to the center axis. In addition, chairs now flank the sides of the new altar platform. Although the nave is quite long, the angle of the pews allows people to see each other better, eliminating the theater effect and creating an impression of the rows of pews opening out to embrace the altar

51. A combination of antiphonal and conventional seating brings people closer to the altar in a long, narrow space.

area. An entirely new dynamic is achieved in this arrangement within a traditional longitudinal shape whose original intention was to support a quite different eucharistic theology.

Given suitable proportions and a scale appropriate for the needed seating capacity, Gothic revival churches congenially lend themselves to beautiful marriages with the new liturgy. The cathedral in Paterson, New Jersey, built in 1870, was renovated in 1987. (Figure 52) A new altar platform thrusts forward with chairs facing from either side. The insistent longitudinal axis and integrity of the

52. The new liturgy finds a congenial home in a Gothic revival building.

Gothic piers and shafts and ribbed vaults have been respected, at the same time enabling an entirely new relationship of the assembly to the liturgical action.

A destructive fire at St. James Catholic Church in Chicago necessitated major repairs. (Figure 53) A liturgical renovation was undertaken at the same time. Here, too, the gathered assembly now surrounds the altar, which is newly positioned in front of the old apse. The disappearance of the complex decorative patterns painted on the walls of the old apse and a new lighting system produce a stunning simplicity that celebrates both

53. A simplification of surfaces highlights the space that now provides a home for the liturgy.

the new liturgy and the old building.

A proposal for another Gothic revival church, St. Luke's in River Forest, Illinois, intends a dramatic relationship between the baptismal font and the altar. The altar will be thrust forward on an octagonal platform echoing the shape of the immersion font at the entrance. (Figure 54) The altar and its platform will be detached from the imposing calvary sculpture and high altar now filling the space behind the altar that faces the people. The calvary group, an over-life-sized image of Christ on the cross flanked by Mary and John,

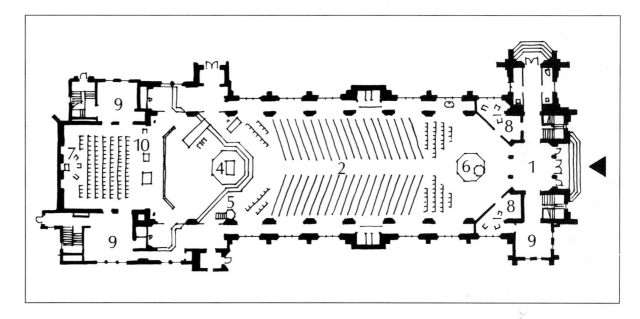

54. A long, narrow space invites a strong axis of altar and font.

1 Gathering
2 Assembly
4 Altar
5 Ambo
6 Baptistry
7 Eucharistic
   reservation
8 Reconciliation
   chapel
9 Sacristy
10 Daily Mass chapel

will be relocated in a devotional area near the baptistry. A large open space will surround the baptistry, allowing for the gathering of people at the font. A corresponding open space will surround the altar, allowing movement and space for funerals and weddings, children's Masses and the enrollment of

catechumens—in other words, room for the community to transact its business.

Generalized Solutions

The renovation of a "temporary" steel gymnasium church is a typical challenge to designers. These buildings, depending on particulars

(load-bearing walls vs. column-beam construction), often accommodate wrap-around concourses for gathering spaces and are usually wide enough to shift to a sidelong axis to bring people closer to the altar from all directions. (Figure 55) Another possibility for a longitudinal gymnasium church is shown in the plan in Figure 56. A new gathering space juts out from the original rectangle. Access is on two sides into the gathering space with egress at an angle into the worship space where seating has been re-oriented to surround the altar. The altar now stands on a polygonal platform along a long side of the original building. If an addition to one of these gymnasium churches is not feasible, an option is to locate the baptistry in the former apse, with the seating then gathered around the altar (as is seen, though not in a gym church, in Figure 42).

Square or polygonal plans also offer several possibilities for locating the altar and, therefore, the action of offering eucharist among the faithful. The platform in Figure 57 is entirely movable. It consists of a number of interlocking modular blocks. The furniture is all movable, allowing for a great number of variations in arrangement.

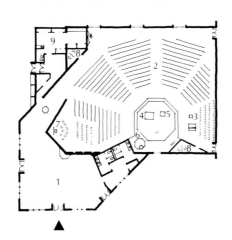

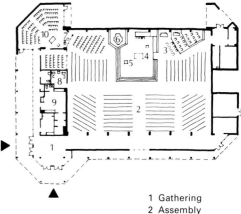

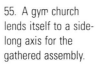

55. A gym church lends itself to a side-long axis for the gathered assembly.

56. A "wrap around" concourse and a new gathering space transform a 1960s box church.

1 Gathering
2 Assembly
3 Music area
4 Altar
5 Ambo
6 Baptistry
7 Eucharistic reservation
8 Reconciliation chapel
9 Sacristy
10 Daily Mass chapel

Refining the Arrangement

Once a seating arrangement has been chosen to best provide an opportunity for the whole community to celebrate eucharist together, additional concerns help to refine that choice. The celebration of eucharist calls for ample room for the procession of ministers as well as movement of the people toward the altar for communion. Is there one center aisle on a direct axis or are there options that would support more than perfunctory

57. A modular platform and movable furniture allow direct and specific responses to varying ritual needs.

entrance processions for eucharist? Is there at least as strong a processional axis from the baptistry to the altar as there is from the sacristy? Does the arrangement of the seating enhance the possibility for ease of movement or does the seating impede movement? If pews are used, do they imprison people, making it easier and thus preferable *not* to move? Do tall, solid-backed pews obstruct the view of children and young people, encouraging inattention? Is there room for wheelchairs to maneuver so that the handicapped do not feel conspicuous and thus less likely to participate? Is there ample room for people to gather up front for anointing services? Is there room for a casket? Is there room for a number of catechumens and their sponsors to gather up front regularly? Does the seating arrangement allow for the easy movement of children (and adults) from their places to con-

verge in a large and open area? Anticipation of freer movement on the part of the assembly will immensely assist in efforts to design for the assembly as the "doers" of liturgy, and a space that allows for movement can't help but encourage such movement! Figure 43 shows two arrangements of an assembly space that anticipates a variety of movement in response to ritual needs.

Important Consequences

One of the earliest consequences of the liturgical reform was the moving forward of the altar so that the presider could face the people. In many cases this meant the addition of a new and thus second altar because the former one was too monumental to bring forward and often had an elaborate reredos.

The impetus for change emerged out of the pastoral con-

cern that the faithful "may be able to unite . . . more closely to the church's prayer, pass over from being simply spectators to becoming active participants." These were Pope Paul VI's words at the March 7, 1965, promulgation of the use of the vernacular in the liturgy.[12] Three months later, in June of the same year, a letter to the presidents of the conferences of bishops noted: "Since 7 March there has been a widespread movement toward celebration facing the people; it has become clear that this practice is the most advantageous pastorally."[13]

In the course of time, the altar as table and place of sacrifice and offering had become subordinate to its function as the base for the tabernacle and exposition of the sacrament. This had persisted so long that hardly any memory survived of the early Christian experience of the bishop's presiding at a movable table facing the assembly.[14] We have now reclaimed this ancient practice.

The Altar

What is the nature of the altar now at the center of the assembly's activity? The altar is a sign of Christ.[15] The tradition also clearly mandates that the altar is a table of both sacrifice and banquet. This dual understanding of the meaning of the altar is emphasized near the beginning of the instruction on the *Rite of Dedication of a Church and an Altar.* The text points out that since the memorial instituted by Christ of his sacrifice to the Father was a sacrificial meal, "Christ made holy the table where the community would come to celebrate their Passover. Therefore the altar is the table for a sacrifice and for a banquet."[16]

Both the sacrificial and banquet aspects of the eucharistic table require recognition and expression. The power of the image of sacrifice lifts up the domesticity of eating and drinking to a banquet experience. Likewise, evoking the dining image of the domestic table tempers unbridled tendencies toward massive sacrificial slabs. A balance and a tension between the two images allows expression of the fullness of the image of Christ. This is what the table signifies, a table made holy by the sacrificial meal offered upon it.

Generally altars made of beautiful wood more effectively evoke the domestic aspects of dining than immobile stone. But the altar as focus of the assembly's activity requires a table distinct from a domestic table. The distinction is partly found in scale. It is clearly a table, but just as clearly invites us to see it with new eyes. Scale does not mean simply wider or longer. It refers to a certain strength, a sta-bility, an honesty, a beauty inherent in its form. (Figure 58) As EACW describes it:

> The altar, the holy table, should be the most beautifully designed and constructed table the community can provide. It is the common table of the assembly, a symbol of the Lord, at which the presiding minister stands and upon which are placed the bread and wine and their vessels and the book. It is holy and sacred to this assembly's action and sharing, so it is never used as a table of convenience or as a resting place for papers, notes, cruets, or anything else. (EACW, 71)

A height somewhat taller than a dining table reveals the duality of the image, assuring that the altar is not just a dining table but a table of sacrifice as well. (Figure 59) As liturgical designer John Buscemi succinctly puts it, "Altars need to be enlarged furniture rather than scaled down architecture." EACW says this of the altar's proportion:

The altar is designed and constructed for the action of a community and the functioning of a single priest—not for concelebrants. The holy table, therefore, should not be elongated, but square or slightly rectangular, an attractive, impressive, dignified, noble table, constructed with solid and beautiful materials, in pure and simple proportions. (EACW, 72)

The Presider's Chair

A prohibition concerning the presider's chair, that "every appearance of a throne should be avoided,"[17] testifies to past experience.

The chair expresses the "office of presiding over the assembly and of directing prayer."[18] In fact, the location of the chair speaks more eloquently than its shape does of the office of presiding over the assembly. After all, it is a human being who presides, not a chair.

Different types of liturgies require some flexibility in the location of the presider's chair.

58. The altar should be a dignified table of noble proportions and of beautiful materials.

59. Scale and form distinguish the altar from other tables.

60. The presider's chair should be dignified but not look like a throne.

The chair should be dignified. (Figures 60 and 61) It should evoke stability and presence, yet not distract from the movement and gestures of the presider. The chair anchors the place from which the celebrant presides, providing a visual assurance of order in the assembly.

The Ambo or Lectern

The placement of the ambo and its dignity as a piece of furniture reflect our understanding of the proclamation of the word of God.

The ambo is essentially a reading desk. (Figure 62) It is not a shrine for the gospel book. As Aidan Kavanagh asserts: "The shrine of the gospel itself is the life of the faithful assembly which celebrates the word liturgically. The gospel book, which is 'sacramental' of all this, is constantly in motion, being carried, held, opened, read from, closed and laid rather than left somewhere behind votive lights or under lock and key."[19] The act of reading the word is more important than the lectern, and the reader should be visible and clearly served by rather than dominated by the furniture. (Figure 63) The lectern makes reverence for the word visible in the beauty of its materials and its form. (Figure 64)

A worthy ambo might be a new reading desk designed to express its public function; or a rich and venerable old ambo might be recrafted by an artist, preserving its presence and history while appropriately serving contemporary needs. In either case, care must be given to unobtrusively accommodating the wiring that is necessary for microphones.

A "movable" item of furniture need not look "temporary." Movability is desirable so that in particular circumstances, such as Morning Prayer or Evening Prayer,

the lectern can assume a central position.

Furniture for the Assembly

There is no question that pews limit and frustrate movement by the assembly. They are solid barriers separating the assembly from

61. An elegant simplicity and beautiful materials provide a worthy chair for the presider.

62. The ambo is essentially a reading desk.

64. Reverence for the word is made visible in beautiful materials and form.

63. The lectern should not overshadow the reader.

the presider and other ministers, encouraging a passive observation. They hamper easy formation of processions involving the whole assembly, and their placement inevitably limits or prohibits gathering around the baptismal font. In older churches pews sometimes carry with them connotations of class and rank and privilege, as they have "belonged" for generations to particular families. Because they are bolted to the floor, one cannot easily open up certain areas to free space for occasions when the assembly needs to gather or move in special ways. The placement of chairs in several front rows offers the opportunity to accommodate weddings, funerals and movement at all liturgies. (Figure 65)

The limitations imposed by pews can be reduced if the ends of the pews are open (ends "box" the people into the rows) and if there are no "modesty panels" or railings

65. Movable seating near centers of liturgical action overcomes some of the limits of fixed pews.

with kneelers on the front rows surrounding the altar. (Figure 66) These panels and railings serve as effectively as the old altar railing to fence the people out of the space occupied by the ministers. The image of the worship space is to be

66. Open ends on pews do not box people in.

a single room; only then can the assembly cease to be an audience. There is no need to consider pews constitutive of a worship space— they are a modern invention introduced essentially for the elderly and the infirm. Even today many European churches have no pews at all and only a few dozen chairs for those physically unable to stand for the duration of a liturgy.

Movable seating offers the most advantages for public worship. In fact, EACW refers only to benches or chairs (never to pews) in its discussion of furnishing for liturgical celebration (EACW, 68). Two things should be kept in mind. First, it is unlikely that seating will be rearranged every Sunday. It is rearranged to facilitate the most effective gathering of the assembly (given the varying numbers at different rites), to invite the dignity and fullness of experience each event deserves. Second, "movable" does not have to mean gray steel folding chairs that will stay in a perpetual disarray in the worship space. Sturdy, handsome seats, either upholstered or solid wood, lock in orderly arrangements (satisfying fire codes in public buildings) and are comfortable and beautiful. A church will look no less a church for having handsome seats whose movability honors the needs of the community's ritual life. (Figure 67)

The Tabernacle

If the celebration of eucharist is the summit toward which all the church's activity is directed and the fount from which all its power flows, then the privilege of participation at eucharist belongs to all members of the community. The tabernacle stands as a sign of the willingness to extend the assembly's worship to those not able to be there. The body of Christ offered and shared at the community's wor-

67. Movable seating can be beautiful, comfortable and dignified.

ship is reserved for the sick and dying, that they too might participate in the great hymn of praise and thanksgiving to the Creator.

The celebration and reservation of the eucharist represent two separate realities. The worship space is designated and designed for the action of the celebration of eucharist; the place of reservation of the eucharist serves the need of the community's ministry to the sick and dying. In addition, it meets personal devotional needs. (Figures 47, 48, 54 and 56) Both EACW and the Bishops' Committee on the Liturgy document concerning eucharistic reservation emphasize the need to have a separate place of reservation because

active and static aspects of the same reality cannot claim the same human attention at the same time. Having the eucharist reserved in a place apart does not mean it has been relegated to a secondary place of no importance. Rather, a space carefully designed and appointed can give

proper attention to the reserved sacrament. (EACW, 78)

The Bishops' Committee on the Liturgy, in keeping with the recommendation in the *General Instruction of the Roman Missal* (277), urges that the place of reservation clearly be separate from the space reserved for the celebration of eucharist. Particularly in situations where additional spaces are not available, such as in some renovations of older buildings, the document counsels: "Such separation need not always be interpreted spatially by walls and barriers, but can also be creatively rendered by other means of spatial definition (e.g., materials employed, use of lighting, etc.).[20]

Given the relationship of the reserved sacrament to the assembly's celebration of eucharist, several other principles, in addition to a separate location for the tabernacle, become evident. For

example, an altar does not provide an appropriate base for the tabernacle. The altar is a place for the activity of the offering of the sacrificial meal. The reserved sacrament is an expression of that completed action. Thus the tabernacle more properly stands on its own pedestal (Figure 68) or in a tower, or is placed in a wall niche. (Figure 69) Its image should be one of a diaconal readiness for the ministry of Christ's care.

68. A pedestal is an appropriate support for a tabernacle.

69. The eucharist may be reserved in a wall-mounted tabernacle.

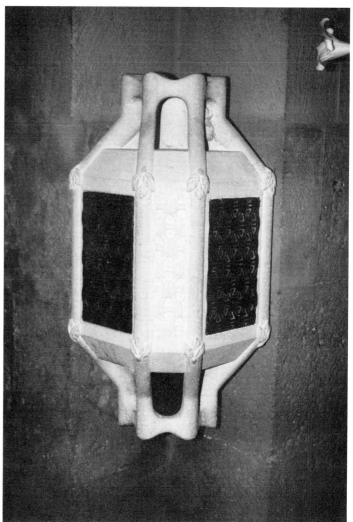

Notes:

1. Paul Engle, "An Iowa Christmas," reprinted in *A Christmas Treasury*, ed. Jack Newcombe (New York: The Viking Press, 1982), 147–54.

2. *Mystici Corporis*, 1. Selections from this document and from *Mediator Dei* are quoted in *Official Catholic Teachings: Worship and Liturgy*, ed. James J. Megivern (Wilmington, North Carolina: McGrath Publishing Co., 1978).

3. *Mystici Corporis*, 82, 58. "In this act of sacrifice through the hands of the priest, by whose word alone the Immaculate Lamb is present on the altar, the faithful themselves, united with him in prayer and desire, offer to the Eternal Father a most acceptable victim of praise and propitiation for the needs of the whole church."

4. *Mediator Dei*, 86.

5. *Mediator Dei*, 87.

6. *Mediator Dei*, 88. "Nor is it to be wondered at, that the faithful should be raised to this dignity. By the waters of baptism, as by common right, Christians are made members of the Mystical Body of Christ the Priest, and by the 'character' which is imprinted on their souls, they are appointed to give worship to God. Thus they participate, according to their condition, in the priesthood of Christ."

7. *Dogmatic Constitution on the Church* (*Lumen Gentium*), 11. "Taking part in the eucharistic sacrifice, the fount and apex of the whole Christian life, they offer the divine victim to God and offer themselves along with him. Thus by reason of both the offering and holy communion all take part in the liturgical service, not indeed all in the same way, but all in their proper way. Strengthened in holy communion by the body of Christ, they then manifest in a concrete way the unity of the people of God that this sacrament aptly signifies and wondrously causes."

8. *Dogmatic Constitution on the Church*, 10.

9. Monika K. Hellwig, "Holy Places in Christian Theology," *Liturgy* (Fall 1983), 13.

10. Nathan Mitchell, "The Sense of the Sacred," *Parish: A Place for Worship*, ed. Mark Searle (Collegeville: The Liturgical Press, 1980), 69.

11. Ann Perkins, *The Art of Dura-Europos* (Oxford: The Clarendon Press, 1973), 29.

12. Paul VI, remarks at the Angelus to the people in St. Peter's Square, on the beginning of the vernacular in the liturgy, 7 March 1965, in *Documents on the Liturgy*, 114.

13. Letter *Le renouveau liturgique* of Cardinal G. Lercaro to presidents of the conferences of bishops on furthering liturgical reform, 30 June 1965, in *Documents on the Liturgy*, 120.

14. Theodor Klauser, *A Short History of the Western Liturgy*, Second Edition (Oxford: Oxford University Press, 1979), 143.

15. Decree *Dedicationis Ecclesiae*, May 29, 1977, in *Documents on the Liturgy*, 1368.

16. Instruction, *Rite of Dedication of a Church and Altar*, chapter 4, paragraph 3, in *Documents on the Liturgy*, 114.

17. *General Instruction of the Roman Missal*, 271.

18. Ibid.

19. Aidan Kavanagh, *Elements of Rite* (New York: Pueblo Publishing Company, Inc., 1982), 18.

20. Bishops' Committee on the Liturgy, *Study Text 11: Eucharistic Worship and Devotion Outside Mass* (Washington, D.C.: United States Catholic Conference, 1987), 60.

CHAPTER **6**

Art in the Service of Worship

The Role of Decor

Here we wish only to recognize the importance of any objects placed within the house for the church and argue that such objects be imbued with artistic merit and contribute to the worship. It is not so much that our buildings or furniture require enhancement, but our spirits cry out to be lifted up, consoled, joyously encountered by the divine, the holy. The role of all decor is to enhance the worship of the gathered assembly.

Worship and Devotion

Both the permanent works of art that belong to the community and the temporary decor must attend to two distinct sets of needs: the worship of the whole assembly and the personal devotion of individuals. The primary places belong to those elements that affect the communal worship. The focal points are the assembly, font, ambo, table and presider's chair. Nothing ought to challenge these priorities. Images of the saints and of biblical and other stories, stations of the cross, vigil lights and other objects for devotion should not divert attention. Their location should be subordinate to the liturgical activities of the assembly.[1]

These activities center on Sunday eucharist. However, other community celebrations—weddings, funerals, various rites relating to initiation, reconciliation services and the Liturgy of the Hours prayed as Morning Prayer and Evening Prayer—are to be taken into account. The worship space should be unencumbered enough that any communal act of worship can be celebrated with integrity of focus.

Cross

During a building renovation process, discussions of the scale and location of a cross are often animated. The *General Instruction of the Roman Missal* (270) states explicitly: "There is also to be a cross, clearly visible to the congregation, either on the altar or near it." Contemporary practice is to keep the altar clear of everything but the necessary bread, wine and sacramentary (EACW, 88). Our tradition is that a cross should be carried in procession to begin our worship. This, rather than a permanent piece of sculpture, serves the liturgy. Its presence seems to attest that this assembly is now in session. Giving priority of place to the processional cross (Figure 70) does not diminish reverence for the notion of sacrifice. It rather shifts the attention to the active celebration of the sacrifice of Christ.

None of the documents requires that the cross be furnished with a corpus. The cross is an image of the entire paschal mystery —Christ's passover and our own. The crucifix is something different, one artist's representation of one moment in the unfolding of that paschal mystery. Even when done well, this limits the image.

The *General Instruction of the Roman Missal* urges that the cross carried in the procession be placed near the altar to serve as the cross of the altar. If another cross is permanently in the presider's area, the processional cross should be put away during the service (Appendix to the *General Instruction*, 270). The document points out that the symbolism of the cross is not served by duplication of the image. Often a crucifix that has served as a backdrop for the altar can be relocated in an area for private prayer. This is usually a pleasing solution.

Art Glass

Art glass ("stained glass") is among the most loved of the repertory of ecclesiastical imagery. Art glass is a means of expression, of communication. It can add immeasurably to the meaning of a space. The inclusion of art glass represents a serious financial as well as aesthetic commitment. The commissioning of an artist should be made with all the care with which an architect is selected. This artist should collaborate with the architect from the project's early stages so that a unity of style can be achieved.

The function of art glass should be clearly understood. For example, the transformation of light quality in the baptistry, reservation chapel, reconciliation chapel or gathering area merits consideration. However, a glass wall behind the altar or even flanking the altar is often a visual distraction in its intensity and can limit visibility of the altar area because of the bright backlighting condition.

70. A processional cross of significant scale and beauty serves the liturgy.

71. The beauty of stained glass can draw the daily
life of a community into their prayer.

The role and purpose of art glass have changed over its history, as have the techniques and materials employed. The glory of glass's transparency and translucency lies in its capacity to interpret and express complex ideas and feelings in ways that vary according to the exterior light quality, weather and seasons of the year. Glass design offers unparalleled opportunities to acknowledge local realities such as landscapes or occupations or flora and fauna.

The design in Figure 71 is St. Ann's Church, Glace Bay, Nova Scotia. It recalls the coal mine shafts that are the principal source of employment in that town. Thus glass offers a way to praise God and to pray for this larger world. The imagery and color, subtleties and intensity of glass can draw the human and ordinary to the divine. It is a medium of transformation. When used with discretion, it is a medium for expression of Christian experience.

Liturgical and Religious Art

A critical distinction is to be made between artifacts that serve the assembly in liturgy and other art that may be called "religious." The latter covers all the works of art that are not for use in the liturgy but may still find a home in the church—as they may in homes and other places. Usually the subject matter is what makes the work religious art. The work itself may be fine art, folk art or something between, but if it is for public display, it should be worthy of being called "art." It has long been the practice to have some amount of religious art in our place of worship. This is still appropriate as long as the art is worthy, does nothing to distract from the liturgy and serves to challenge, to console, to enrich the faithful.[2]

All good art engages the viewer in an active way, inviting the viewer to enter into the reality to which it alludes. Ranging from exuberant and animated to quiet and contemplative, it is evocative and provocative because its core lies in human experience, meeting the viewer where the holy dwells.

An example of the demands we must make on religious art might center on an image of St. Monica. An artist commissioned to produce a statue of St. Monica would first ask, "Who was St. Monica and does she speak to us today?" That artist, besides discovering that she was the mother of St. Augustine, might become fascinated with the fact that she was a recovered alcoholic, that she endured great emotional suffering through the years of her son's heresy as a Manichaen, that she persevered in prayer for his eventual conversion. Hers is the story of a mother who loved her son in spite of his wayward youth. She believed in prayer and she trusted God.

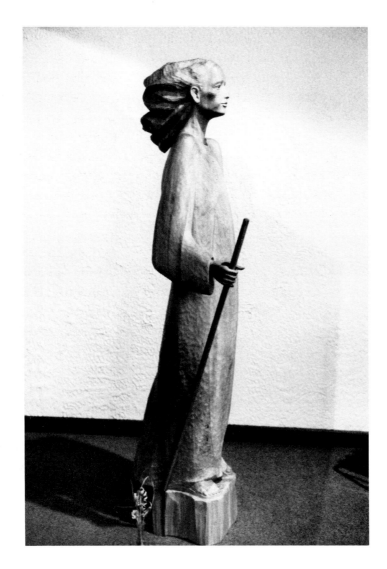

72. A modern sculpture of St. Monica reminds us of this mother's pain and care and her steadfast trust in God.

Such a woman has a great deal to offer twentieth-century people, beset by the same afflictions of alcohol and chemical abuse, worried sick about their children. The image of such a woman should evoke a steadfast courage and perseverance, a strength of purpose coming from trust in God's mercy and God's providence. (Figure 72) The image of such a woman probably shouldn't be sweet and lovely, but rather solid and straightforward, head held high. Here is a sculpture to meet at ground level, a woman to meet in our midst. She stands among us, sharing across the centuries the vicissitudes always and everywhere of being caught up in the pain of being human while at the same time rejoicing in God's redemption.

That participation in the profound reality of the subject satisfies deep human needs. Since the time of the earliest extant examples in

Christianity, in about the sixth century, images have invited an entering into the reality to which they refer—a kind of participation for which our spirits still yearn. Those needs call for opportunities to encounter saints in whose communion we believe. Such images can be two- or three-dimensional, of wood, of stone, of bronze, of fiber or fabric, or of any other material, permanent or temporary, whatever is appropriate to touch people's sensibilities.

The imagery in our places of worship should engage the human spirit and console and gladden our hearts. Art should enrich our places of worship, giving them warmth and spirit. In our efforts to overcome the excesses of an earlier piety and to help people move toward new understandings of themselves as the celebrants of liturgy, we can easily forget that our heritage for centuries has been one of reverence for the beautiful and a respect for the creative gifts of artists in our churches. As we explore and reclaim earlier understandings of being church, of celebrating our ritual life together and being formed by it, let us also remember and reclaim our need for the beautiful and a reverence before those simple and honest and authentic things that help us know and celebrate our identity as the body of Christ.

The Artifacts for Liturgy

Vessels are to reflect their function for drinking or nurturing fire, for disclosing the generosity of the community's oils for anointing (Figure 73), for containing the holy waters of baptism. They will be of a scale so that they are "legible" in the assembly.

Vesture will enhance the gestures of the ministers, make visible the movements that order and lead the assembly. Vestments are not signboards. They do not need signs and symbols on them. They need to be of beautiful fabrics capable of moving, flowing with and emphasizing gestures.

Textiles and fiber art have a magnificent potential to contribute, but are among the most abused of all the media. Hangings, for example, are not sewn-up, two-dimensional flatwork. As with vestments, fabric and fiber images should not be signboards. They can be three-dimensional, sometimes even like sculpture. And they need not always hang on a wall. They can hang where they move freely. They can create an area with its own character. Fabric designs for altar paraments and other furniture invite new and more appropriate solutions; their design and use has often been inappropriate.

In addition to the altar, ambo and presider's chair, there are other

73. Beautiful vessels manifest reverence for the community's oils.

74. A well-crafted music stand contributes to the dignity of the liturgy.

furnishings that contribute to liturgy—music stands (Figure 74), candle stands, the paschal candle, tables for the eucharistic gifts, flower pedestals, the base for a processional cross, vigil light for the place of eucharistic reservation. These may all be crafted specifically for a given parish.

Note:

1. See the *Directory on the Pastoral Ministry of Bishops (Ecclesiae imago)*, 22 February 1973, 91, in *Documents on the Liturgy 1963–1979* (Collegeville: The Liturgical Press, 1982), 838. Also, *The Code of Canon Law* (New York: Paulist Press, 1985), Canon 1188: "The practice of displaying sacred images in the churches for the veneration of the faithful is to remain in force; nevertheless they are to be exhibited in moderate number and in suitable order lest they bewilder the Christian people and give opportunity for questionable devotion."

2. James F. White and Susan J. White briefly address this distinction in their book, *Church Architecture, Building and Renovating for Christian Worship* (Nashville: Abingdon Press, 1988), 154–62. For a related discussion see Paul Tillich, "Existentialist Aspects of Modern Art," in *Christianity and the Existentialists*, ed. Carl Michalson (New York: Charles Scribner's Sons, 1956), 128–47.

EPILOGUE

Shaping a House for the Church: Other Contributing Factors

This book primarily addresses the conceptual level of designing an appropriate place for worship. The model proposed is that of the ritual activities, their relationship to each other, and their formative role in the community's life. A successful church building or renovation project also includes attention to the following issues:

INTERIOR

Acoustics. Hearing each other in word and song as well as hearing the presider, lector and cantor.

Heating, ventilation, cooling. Physical comfort, aesthetics, stewardship, noise, cost, delivery system coordination.

Safety and fire codes. Egress, doors and windows, materials, seating configuration constraints, cost.

Structural design. Free/clear spans, sizes, aesthetics, materials, cost.

EXTERIOR

Parking. Proximity, size, flow, environmental impact, vegetation / landscape design.

Site and context. Character, stewardship, environmental impact, scale, indigenous materials and geography, planting design.

Climate and environment. Compatibility with the "place," orientation, materials, exposures.

PROCESS

This hidden factor affects all aspects of a project. Who are the members of the building/project team? How is the team selected? How do members do their work and how do they interact with the community as well as to each other?

Process components include: listening, communication, coordination, reflection, goal-setting, responding, sharing, scheduling, technical/non-technical integration, cash-flow planning, long-range financial planning, facility audits and evaluations.

LIST OF ILLUSTRATIONS

Drawings are by Armando Garzon-Blanco. Unless otherwise indicated, photographs are by Marchita B. Mauck. Floor plans of modern churches are by Bill Beard.

24. 333 Wacker Drive, Chicago. (Photo, Antonio Pérez.)

25. Parking garage, Torpedo Factory Condominiums, Alexandria, Virginia. (Metcalf & Associates, and Keyes, Condon, & Florance. Photo, Dorothy Shawhan.)

26. St. Thomas More Church, Baton Rouge, Louisiana. (Clifton C. Lasseigne, AIA, and Walter E. Legett, Jr., AIA, Architects Incorporated; Marchita B. Mauck, Liturgical Design Consultant.)

27. Prince of Peace Lutheran Church of the Deaf, St. Paul, Minnesota. (Ralph Rapson and Associates, Inc., Minneapolis, Minnesota. Photo, courtesy of Ralph Rapson.)

28. St. Cyril of Alexandria Church, Houston, Texas.

29. San Juan Bautista Mission Church, California.

30. S. Maria della Pace Church, Rome, Italy. Designed by Pietro da Cortona, 1656.

31. S. Andrea al Quirinale Church, Rome, Italy. Designed by Bernini, 1658.

32. S. Carlo alle Quattro Fontane Church, Rome, Italy. Designed by Borromini, 1638.

33. Baptistry, Grado, Italy.

34. Baptismal font, baptistry, Grado, Italy.

35. St. Charles Borromeo Church, London, England. (Photo, courtesy of Alan Fudge and Raymond Topley.)

36. Baptismal font, Sacred Heart of Jesus Church, Manvel, Texas. (Photo, courtesy of Don Neumann.)

37. Baptistry, Christ the King Church, South Bend, Indiana. (Richard J. Conyers, Consultant.)

38. Baptistry, St. Cecilia Church, Houston Texas.

39. St. George Church, Baton Rouge, Louisiana. (Raymond Post, AIA, Architects, Baton Rouge, Louisiana.)

40. Baptismal font, St. George Church, Baton Rouge, Louisiana. (Photo, Rocky Baltazar.)

41. St. Bernard Church, Thief River Falls, Minnesota. (Bill Brown AIA Professional Corporation, Colorado Springs.)

42. St. Clement Church, Chicago. (Walker C. Johnson, AIA, Holabird and Root, Chicago.)

43. Our Lady of Perpetual Help Church, Belle Chasse, Louisiana. (William L. Argus, Jr., AIA, Argus Architects; Marchita B. Mauck, Liturgical Design Consultant.)

44. Pre−Vatican II celebration of eucharist.

45. St. Patrick Church, Baton Rouge, Louisiana. (William C. Burks, AIA.)

46. St. Benedict Motherhouse Chapel, St. Joseph, Minnesota. (Frank Kacmarcik, Liturgical Design Consultant. Photo, courtesy of Sisters of St. Benedict.)

47. Light of the World Church, Littleton, Colorado. (Hoover Berg Desmond, Architect, Denver, Colorado; John Buscemi, Liturgical Design Consultant.)

48. Our Lady of Mount Carmel, Newport News, Virginia. (George Yu, Architect; Andrew Ciferni, Liturgical Design Consultant.)

49. Madonna della Strada Chapel, Loyola University, Chicago, Illinois, (Photo, Conrad Schmitt Studios.)

50. St. Thomas More University Parish Church, Norman, Oklahoma. (W. H. Raymond Yeh, FAIA. Photo, courtesy of Raymond Yeh.)

51. St. Bernard Church, Omaha, Nebraska. (William J. Woeger, Liturgical Design Consultant. Photo, courtesy of William Woeger.)

52. Cathedral of St. John the Baptist, Paterson, New Jersey. (Willy Malarcher, Liturgical Design Consultant. Photo, courtesy of Willy Malarcher.)

53. St. James Church, Chicago, Illinois. (Paul Straka, Architect. Photo, Paul Straka.)

54. St. Luke Church, River Forest, Illinois. (John C. Voosen, Architect; Marchita B. Mauck, Liturgical Design Consultant.)

55. Our Lady Mother of the Church, Chicago, Illinois. (John C. Voosen, Architect.)

56. St. George Church, Baton Rouge, Louisiana. (Raymond Post, AIA.)

57. St. Patrick Church, Baton Rouge, Louisiana. (William C. Burks, AIA.)

58. Altar, Madonna della Strada Chapel, Loyola University, Chicago, Illinois. (Designed and built by Eugene Geinzer.)

59. Altar, Sts. Peter and Paul Cathedral, Indianapolis, Indiana. (Edward Sovik, designer.)

60. Presider's chair, William Keyser. Photo, Robert Kushner and Toby Thompson, courtesy of William Keyser.)

61. Presider's chair, Thomas Moser Cabinetmakers. (Photo, courtesy of Thomas Moser.)

62. Reading desk, Thomas Moser Cabinetmakers. (Photo, courtesy of Thomas Moser.)

63. Ambo, William Keyser. (Photo, Robert Kushner and Toby Thompson, courtesy of William Keyser.)

64. Ambo, St. Raphael Cathedral, Dubuque, Iowa. (John Buscemi, Liturgical Design Consultant.)

65. Chairs, St. Alphonsus Church, Greendale, Wisconsin. (Photo, courtesy Frank Ulrich, Sauder Manufacturing Company.)

66. Bench, St. Patrick Church, Colorado Springs. (Modern Fixture Company, Denver.)

67. Upholstered chairs for the assembly, Sts. Peter and Paul Cathedral, Indianapolis, Indiana. Romweber Furniture Co., Inc., Batesville, Indiana. (Edward Sovik, designer.)

68. Tabernacle, St. Maximilian Kolbe Church, Houston, Texas. Candace Knapp, artist. (Photo, courtesy of Don Neumann.)

69. Wall tabernacle, Mainz Cathedral, Mainz, Germany.

70. Processional Cross, Jugenddorf Klinge, Seckach, West Germany.

71. Stained glass windows, St. Ann's Church, Glace Bay, Nova Scotia. Lighthaus Glass, Madison, Wisconsin.

72. Statue, St. Monica Church, Chicago, Illinois. Jerzy Kenar, sculptor.

73. Oils, St. Maximilian Kolbe Church, Houston, Texas. Handblown oil vessels, Fire Island Glass Studio, Austin, Texas. (Photo, courtesy of Don Neumann.)

74. Music stand, William Keyser. (Photo, David J. Leveille, courtesy of William Keyser.)